Humour at the Workplace

Marco Sampietro is a professor at SDA Bocconi School of Management, Italy, and at Mumbai International School of Business (MISB), India. He is also a contract professor at Bocconi University and Milano Fashion Institute, both in Italy. He has authored, co-authored and edited six management books and contributed to more than ten. His interest in humour from a scientific perspective began during his PhD, where he studied the use and effects of humour in international teams. Since then, he regularly studies and observes humour at the workplace.

Humour at the Workplace

Marco Sampietro

RUPA

Published by
Rupa Publications India Pvt. Ltd 2017
7/16, Ansari Road, Daryaganj
New Delhi 110002

Sales centres:
Allahabad Bengaluru Chennai
Hyderabad Jaipur Kathmandu
Kolkata Mumbai

Copyright © Marco Sampietro 2017

The views and opinions expressed in this book are the author's own and the facts are as reported by him which have been verified to the extent possible, and the publishers are not in any way liable for the same.

All rights reserved.
No part of this publication may be reproduced, transmitted, or stored in a retrieval system, in any form or by any means, electronic, mechanical, photocopying, recording or otherwise, without the prior permission of the publisher.

ISBN: 978-81-291-4526-0

First impression 2017

10 9 8 7 6 5 4 3 2 1

Printed at HT Media Ltd, Noida

This book is sold subject to the condition that it shall not, by way of trade or otherwise, be lent, resold, hired out, or otherwise circulated, without the publisher's prior consent, in any form of binding or cover other than that in which it is published.

For
*My daughter Sienna, the baby I have seen smiling the most.
And my wife Valentina, who always laughs with me
(hopefully, not at me...)*

Contents

Foreword ix
Introduction xv

1. Humour in Our Lives 1
2. The Origin and Evolution of Humour 7
3. Defining Humour (or, at least trying to do so) 12
4. Why Do We Laugh? 15
5. Individual Differences in Humour 27
6. Humour Styles 36
7. Humour in India 45
8. Are Workplaces Funny Places? Are They Looking for Humour? 49
9. Organizational Culture and Humour 55
10. Patterns of Humour at the Workplace 58
11. Types of Humour at the Workplace 64
12. The Positive Side of Humour at the Workplace 76

13. The Dark Side of Humour at the Workplace 127
14. Working in International Environments 133
    with Humour
15. Conclusions and Final Suggestions for the Proper 140
    Implementation of Humour at the Workplace

Bibliography 149

Foreword

When Marco Sampietro asked me to write this foreword, I jumped at the opportunity, because, well, it's a rare kind of work, and I felt almost heroic taking it up—I felt like I was being asked to defend an unsung hero, the kind that would hang around unassumingly in smoke-filled coffee houses in a coat with elbow patches and a golf cap and dark brown glasses, holding a newspaper, waiting to catch the attention of the waitstaff, waiting for the right timing. That's humour. He could be a misfit, he could be silly, he could be just too plain or too tart, but—and there's research to back me up on this—he's the guy the girls go out with. That is evolutionary logic at its best and that's the kind you don't argue with.

Humour is every bit special, it is unlike other human tendencies. It is radical—it is only given to us Homo sapiens, just like speech, imagination, consciousness, and spirituality. It is empowering and endearing. No wonder then, that we make friends with people who make us laugh, fall in love with people who know how to laugh, find it easier to trust people who don't take themselves too seriously, and enjoy working with those who understand the importance of this secret ingredient for a happy life.

To quote P.G. Wodehouse, that master of humour who dignified the slapstick with wry British humour and turned the joke on the unlikeliest theme of the time—the British aristocracy: 'As we grow older and realize more clearly the limitations of human happiness, we come to see that the only real and abiding pleasure in life is to give pleasure to other people.' This tells us another beautiful quality about humour—it is ennobling. An act that can defuse negativity in a situation and transform it into something where people find their synergy towards something positive can only be noble.

Of course, humour is all of these amazing things when it's not targeting someone personally, when it's not flogging the dead horse of an unfair stereotype, when it is deployed at the expense of a situation rather than a person. It has its boundaries, its own form, techniques, and to deploy it needs skill, timing, precision, and at the very least, a personality.

I have an academic background in human resources but thanks to my family's deep involvement in the study of ancient Indian scriptures, a lot of my work and research draws on the leanings and the wisdom of the Indian culture through a study of the Vedas and Upanishads, and two of the most well-known epics—the Ramayana and the Mahabharata. The Sanskrit literature recognizes Hasya (laughter) as one of the nine Rasas (emotions) among—Shringar (love), Adbhuta (wonder), Shanta (peace), Raudra (anger), Veera (courage), Karuna (compassion), Bhayanak (fear) and Vibhatsa (disgust).

What makes ancient Sanskrit works unique is their ability to explore, discuss, and as it turns out, laugh.

I would like to offer this little piece of humour that forms a part of a collection of Sanskrit Subhashitani (good sayings), that seeks to take a lighter view of the most powerful and the most revered of a trinity of deities in the Hindu pantheon—Brahma (the Creator), Vishnu (the Preserver) and Mahesh (Shiva, the Destroyer):

कमनेब्रह्माशेतेहर: शेतेहिमालये।
क्शीरब्धौचहरि: शेतेमन्येमत्कुणशन्कय।।

Brahma sleeps on a lotus, Shiva sleeps in Himalaya, Vishnu sleeps in Ksheersaagar—it's all due to the fear of bugs in their bed!

The imagery of these deities is replete with symbolism—lotus symbolizes purity, Himalaya stands for strength and the Ksheersaagar means the ocean of milk.

For me, personally, there cannot be a more profound statement in favour of humour than when a culture preserves a gem seeking to invoke humour directed at the subject of a deity considered extraordinarily powerful. It is an incredibly humbling gesture.

The Indian culture is full of stories of humour being taken very seriously, from which, perhaps, stemmed the tradition of court jesters whose job it was to hold up a mirror to the ruler of a realm. They not only made the king laugh, they could also be said to have almost governed the realm through their witticisms: Indian history speaks of stalwarts such as Birbal (one of the nine 'Navratnas (gems)' or ministers of Mughal Emperor Akbar the Great, a friend and confidant of the Emperor, the only one to have been granted an accommodation within the Emperor's palace) and Tenali Raman, a Telegu court-jester and poet, who hailed from the present-day Andhra

Pradesh, in the court of Krishna Deva Raya. I look up to these as instances of humour at workplace and for the most part, they are so inspiring in the way these geniuses deployed it to safeguard a cause for justice, fairness, and knowledge, ensuring that their king took the right step and that he remained humble.

Humour, in the Indian society, is important also as a form of social commentary and social dialogue. In the state of Gujarat, we see a tradition of the Bhavai, wherein the narrator is a couple—a man and a woman, called ranglo and rangli. The root word is 'rang' which means colour, and ranglo (male) and rangli (female) are both genderized versions of the word 'colourful'. The performance of Bhavai is marked by the narrators making witty jabs at the various acts of drama presented in a logical progression and inviting dialogue from onlookers. In Gujarati, they have a proverb that establishes, 'One that laughs, thrives.'

The truth of that wisdom is corroborated in my personal research on leadership as well as spirituality. Happy leaders make for better leaders, and they are also more spiritual. While the directionality of the relationship between spirituality, happiness, and well-being needs to be explored further, it is clear that they are strongly correlated and contribute both to effectiveness and efficiency. This also has implications for business leadership, especially ethical leadership.

Such humour is at once entertaining and insightful, fosters dialogue, and renders workplaces more productive. Exactly what we need more at our workplaces, since they have progressively turned into dark little traps of competition, comparison and insecurity. Not to mention, the fact that we in the developed world have been spending more and more time at work while the digital world has blurred the boundaries between the personal and the professional.

For views, I turned to Rajeev Kapoor, who, as the Director of the Lal Bahadur Shastri National Academy of Administration, the institution that trains the senior bureaucrats of the Indian Civil Services, and who I had the opportunity to observe dealing with the crème de la crème of the Indian bureaucracy with authority and élan, and more so with a great sense of humour. This is what he had to say, 'The only thing which can keep the morale high and tired souls energized at dreary workplaces and especially during long, boring meetings is a touch of light humour...not directed at a person but at the work itself. I have tried it and it works.'

Personal matters, it seems, are the no-go areas, also attested by Anindya Lala, Vice President (VP), Business Planning and Strategy, Essar Steel, in saying, 'Humour at workplaces keeps the atmosphere cordial and ensures no one takes themselves too seriously. Taboo, well, it depends on the maturity level of the team. However, some areas are best left out—appearance, sexual connotations, family background, major professional bloopers and religion.'

I strongly believe that this book will give us all a new dimension to the ongoing discussion on making workplaces more engaging and more humane through humour. In my view, though, humour at the workplace is a very hyperlocalized version of an essentially human desire—to enjoy our time together.

Therefore, the irony of Marco asking an HR professor to write the foreword to his book is not lost on me. Any association that the reader finds with Dilbert, the widely read comic trip on workplace humour, especially the evil human resources director Catbert, would be purely incidental. I say this in all lightness of the subject at hand, but I truly appreciate Marco's work in this direction and look forward to reading more of his work.

Professor Himanshu Rai
Associate Professor of Human Resource Management,
IIM Lucknow
Former Dean, MISB Bocconi and SDA Professor of
Organization & Human Resource Management

Introduction

Without any doubts, humour plays a very important role in our lives: humour supports the cognitive development in newborns and children, humour has a high influence in preferring and selecting friends, we mostly engage with people who make us laugh or appreciate our sense of humour, we enjoy when someone describes us as humorous, we invest a good deal of our time looking for humorous content (books, films, YouTube videos, social media, etc.).

It has been calculated that, on an average, we spend 115 days of our life laughing.

Work is another important component of our lives. On an average, Indians sleep for 528 minutes per night and work for 486 minutes per day. That means that we spend 53 per cent of our waking time working.

The question is: since work absorbs a good part of our lives and humour is a key ingredient of our private lives, is there room for humour in work settings?

In this book we will see that there is room for humour in work settings too, even if less as compared to non-working time. We will also see that humour and work are not opponents, in fact, if properly implemented, humour can even increase the performance of the employees and their well-being. As an appetizer, let us see two examples.

The wise father

A company, due to the poor management of the former CEO, was in turmoil. The main shareholders asked for a meeting with him and the CEO tried to hide the poor performance by making up financial data. The shareholders discovered the reality and they immediately fired him. The former CEO was a very serious person, always ready to show his power and to reprimand his subordinates.

A new CEO was then appointed.

Day 1 of the new CEO: Plenary Meeting.

Even if the employees had never met the new CEO before, they were already scared of him since they believed that he would fire a lot of people and worsen the already bad organizational climate. In addition, in their minds, starting with a plenary meeting meant that the new CEO had to communicate tough decisions.

This negative attitude was instilled by the former CEO, who always blamed his subordinates for the poor performance of the company, when as a matter of fact, he was the real problem.

The new CEO was aware that the company had a lot of potential and that the current issues did not depend on the competencies of the employees. One of the first things he wanted to communicate to his employees was that he was a very approachable person and that the past did not have to influence the future. For this reason, he prepared a strange presentation to be held in front of all his employees.

The new CEO opened the speech by projecting an old picture of him while crying.

He smiled and said, 'This is me when I was 19 years old. My father took this picture. That day my girlfriend had decided to break up with me. She always blamed me for everything wrong that happened in her life. I cried so much that day that I almost died of dehydration. I asked my father why he took a picture of me during that sad moment. He replied, "I will answer in 2 months!"'

The CEO then switched to the next slide. The slide showed him, still young, laughing with a much distorted facial expression. Employees silently laughed. He added, 'My father took this picture 2 months after the break up. He came to me showing this picture, and said, "This is the reason why I took a picture 2 months ago! 2 months ago you were hopeless, now you are more joyful and stronger than before!" After his words, I started crying again and my father added, "Okay, let us try again, let us take another picture…'

Meanwhile, the assistant of the CEO took a picture of the attendees before the speech started and after the last sentence of what the CEO had said. The CEO then projected the last picture and said, 'These are you a few seconds ago, laughing.' He then projected the first picture, 'These are you 2 minutes ago, very serious and sad faces. I believe it is time to smile again in this company!"

All the employees applauded for several minutes.

In this case, humour produced different results: grabbed

the attention of the attendees, reduced their stress levels, reduced the perceived distance between the CEO and the employees, and boosted their morale.

Please, another one!

Reaching the end of a job interview, the HR person asked a young applicant fresh out of business school: 'And what starting salary are you looking for?' The applicant answered, 'In the neighbourhood of 1 crore a year, depending on the benefits package.'

The interviewer said, 'Well, what would you say to a package of 5 weeks paid vacation, full medical and dental insurance, and a company car leased every 2 years, say…a Range Rover Sport?'

The applicant sat up straight and said, 'Wow! Are you kidding?'

The interviewer: 'Yes, but you started it!'

This case is completely opposite to the previous one. In this scenario, humour was used to convey a negative message but instead of 'insulting' the arrogant applicant, he decided to play with him. For sure, the message still arrived loud and clear.

In order to fully understand the role and the importance of humour, especially at the workplace, we will start our journey by considering the role of humour in our lives, then we will find out what humour really is (you will discover that defining humour is quite challenging), why we laugh, what are the main individual differences in the sense of humour, whether companies appreciate humour, how humour is normally used in organizations, and what are the positive and negative effects of using humour at the workplace. In particular, we will see the role of humour at the workplace along these dimensions: stress management, creativity and problem solving, test of the acceptable boundaries, ingratiation, leadership, maintaining the status and hierarchy, group identity, climate and cohesion, negotiation, conflict management, motivation, and communication.

Finally, we will also provide a snapshot of how humour at the workplace changes when working in international business environments.

It is worth mentioning that all the contents of this book are based on scientific studies and contributions from prominent scholars, researchers, professors and top managers. In order to give credit to their efforts and contributions to the understanding of such a fascinating topic, many people are directly mentioned in the book, many others can be found in the pretty detailed bibliography at the end of the book (just in case you want to dig deeper into the humour topic).

In addition, in order to translate theories and suggestions into practice, the book contains more than 50 examples of humour at the workplace with explanations.

Marco Sampietro

Humour in Our Lives

Humour and laughter are a universal aspect of human experience. Humour accompanies us almost from the beginning of our lives and until the end. Some people are able to make other people laugh even after their 'departure', think of comedians or even some relatives and friends who made us laugh during their lifetime, and when we think of them, sadness sometimes is concealed by a smile.

From a developmental perspective, the first vocalization of humans is cry but laughter follows quickly after. The first smiles can be seen during the first few days of life without any influence of external stimuli. Actually, they are not really smiles, but just a way to activate facial muscles and expressions. The development of what we call a 'sense of humour' has to wait a little bit longer; it usually begins at about 3–4 months of age, generally as a response to external stimuli coming from other persons. The first form of humour is imitative, namely it replicates facial expressions of other people around the baby, and it's only after some time that the newborn develops the ability to understand humour mechanism and the mythical peekaboo and hide-and-seek are examples of humour development. Babies laugh, on an average, 400 times a day!

It may be worth mentioning that humour is one of the few inborn characteristics of humankind, in fact, even children born deaf and blind are able to develop their own sense of humour.

Humour is global; all cultures and virtually all individuals throughout the world present some sort of humour, even though each form may have its own differences. In addition, though each individual and culture may find different types of humour amusing and acceptable, but the sound of laughter cannot be distinguished among different cultures.

Humour is a fundamentally social phenomenon. It does not mean that if you laugh alone you are insane; it simply means that we laugh and joke much more when we are with other people than when we are alone. The occasions when we do laugh by ourselves are usually connected to memories of watching a comic show, a joke told by a friend, or an amusing experience. This is the reason why it is generally said that humour, nevertheless, has a pseudo-social origin, even when we are by ourselves.

The role that humour plays in everyday life, and especially in social relations, is particularly significant.

Julia Vettin and Dietmar Todt tape-recorded 48 hours of conversation among friends and strangers. They recorded an average of 5.8 bouts of laughter occurring in every 10-minute period of conversation, with a minimum of zero and a maximum of 15 bouts. Interestingly, they found that participants laughed just as frequently with strangers as with friends and the number of bouts appeared to be much higher if compared to the results of other researches, which asked the participants to track record in daily diaries of how much they laughed. This suggests that people tend to take laughing for granted, thus they often underestimate it because of its 'normality'. It seems that humour is like breathing: it simply happens even if you are not focused on making it happen.

Humour plays a critical role when it comes to interpersonal relations. When people meet for the first time, a humour-based approach helps in reducing the anxiety linked to the uncertainty of the beginning of a human relationship and thus facilitating the formation of interpersonal bonds. Moreover, generally speaking, we are more attracted to people who have a sense of humour. An interesting experiment, related to this topic, was conducted by Arnei Cann, Lawrence Calhoun and Janet Banks. In that experiment, participants were asked to tell a joke to a stranger. Strangers had been instructed to laugh or not laugh at the joke. Participants were also given some information about the person to whom they would have to tell the joke. In certain cases, the information provided evidenced for shared interests and beliefs between the two people, while in others they were of opposite views. Participants were then asked to give an opinion on the person they had just met. This resulted, as forecasted, in higher grades for strangers who laughed at the joke told and who presented common interests and visions with the participants. Interestingly, though, of the 2 combinations—shared interests and no laugh; and no common interests and laugh—the latter prevailed, suggesting that humour has a high attraction power compared to having common interests.

Humour is strongly sought in interpersonal relations, both in friendships or love affairs. Susan Sprecher and Pamela Regan surveyed 700 people, both men and women, about their preferences for a number of attributes they look for in a person depending on the situation such as a casual sex partner, dating partner, spouse, same-sex friend, and other-sex friend. Having a good sense of humour was among the most desirable traits, regardless of the type of relationship. Nevertheless, there exists difference between men and women. Many studies suggest that women pay more attention to the humour trait in the partner than men do, while men—even though they considered it to be very important—often regard beauty as more important.

In 2015, the *Men's Health* magazine commissioned a research in order to, as stated by the magazine, 'identify, quantify, and rank the traits that make a man "hot" to women'. They surveyed more than 1,000 women aged between 21–54 in 2 online polls. One was conducted by Opinion Research Corporation, based in Princeton, New Jersey, and the other was done on the website bestlifeonline.com. They measured 20 variables related to 4 different traits: character, personality, practical skills, and physical attributes. Humour scored first in the personality traits, reporting 77 per cent of the preferences. In general, humour was reported as the second desirable trait, being faithful as the first (84 per cent).

Humour, thus, plays a fundamental role in creating human relationships. What is more complex is to understand if it is enough to sustain those relationships. John Rust, Jeffrey Goldstein, Avner Ziv and Orit Gadish found that the more the couples were satisfied with their relationships, the more they said their partner possesses a good sense of humour. Avner Ziv found that married couples seem to attribute the success of their marriage, among other things, to the humour and laughter they share. During a study on couples married for over 50 years, Robert Lauer, Janet Lauer and Sarah Kerr found that one of the main reasons that people gave for the longevity of the marriage was laughing together often. One question, however, remained unanswered: do we laugh together because we are happy together or are we happy together because we laugh together?

Gottman and Strombom tried to answer that question. What they discovered is that:

- The use of humour by the husband during critical conflicts has a higher probability to lead the couple to separation. In these cases, in fact, humour is not used as a way to ease the problem, but instead as an escape route from the problem itself. If the problem is linked to fundamental aspects of the couple's life, it will come back to undermine the relationship.
- When a wife uses humour in a conflict discussion this may bring more stability for the couple, but only if it is associated with a decrease in the husband's heart rate. We are not suggesting to monitor the heart rate of your husband with some wearable technology, just saying that humour by itself, without any distinction, does not guarantee the successful resolution of an intense discussion with your partner.

Finally, a warning for the humour 'at all costs' lovers; when there is too much use of humour, it lets a partner think that the relationship is not being taken seriously, they may even think that—since humour can be a reason for interpersonal attraction and can be used as a facilitator for meeting new partner—people, especially humoristic people, do not tend to truly commit themselves into a relationship, particularly, when it passes through a hard time, mainly because the search for a new partner for them is not so demanding.

To summarize, it seems that humour really is a part of human nature and drives part of our choices when it comes to selecting the people with whom we prefer to have a relationship. In addition, when it comes to selecting our daily activities, humour plays an important role. The comic industry is always flourishing: the almost infinite number of movies, radio programs, TV series, live shows, books with humour content testify that people enjoy humour.

For example, in November 2015, the Facebook page with most number of likes in India in the community category was 'Laughing Colours', with almost 15 million fans. It was also (again in the community category) the fastest growing page. At the end of October 2015, *Mrs Funnybones* was in the top 10 of the most sold books on www.amazon.in. In the list of the top 20 Indian films, there are 3 films in which humour plays a major role. Among them, *3 Idiots* (2009) was the most successful (ranking 6 in the overall list). It became one of the few Indian films that gained a major success in East Asian markets such as China, eventually bringing its overseas total to more than US$65 million, the highest-grossing Bollywood film of all time in overseas markets, before being overtaken by *Chennai Express* (2013). Finally, on YouTube it is quite common to find Indian funny videos with more than 5 million views.

The Origin and Evolution of Humour

The word 'humour' is derived from the Latin word 'humourem' meaning fluid or liquid. Even today, the term or humour is used to indicate, in specific contexts, some kind of body fluids, such as the vitreous humour. Hippocrates, considered the father of western medicine, believed that the health of human beings was based on the balance of the 4 body fluids or humours. Even Galen, the physician, introduced the idea that the 4 body fluids might have a psychological impact as well as an influence on people's character. For example, an excess of black bile was said to cause a melancholy state and depression. Besides this basic state, it was believed that a variation in the balance of the four humours also influenced the emotional state of a person.

Few realize that the term humour has common semantic roots with the famous rasa of Sanskrit aesthetics. Latin humour and Vedic rasas in their primary meanings both signify the essential liquid element. Also rasas figured in the notions of health, but unlike the Latin humourem, there are 6 rasas. This curious parallelism does not end here, humourem and rasaa find their way into the fine arts, via, it seems, the same route: drama.

In the West, certain character types came to be seen in terms of the imbalance of the 4 essential 'fluids'. A humorous character was, therefore, one in which a specific humourem predominated.

In India, the 'medical' rasas reached drama via a culinary detour: 6 characteristic tastes of food (sweet, sour, etc.) came to be associated with the 6 bodily fluids; it is these tastes that analogically undergird Bharata's 8 dramatic flavours—love, pity, disgust, etc., which the drama combines into a unique and pleasing blend, just as a good cook does with his ingredients. The paths of humour and rasaa do diverge at a certain point. On the Indian side, we see no conflation of humour with the comic sensibility. In its aesthetic sense, rasaa remains a humour in the larger sense only. But even here, the comic (hasya) is counted as one of the 8 primary rasas.

In Europe, as early as the 16th century, the term humour does not have any connotation of amusement or laughter, even though its link with the emotional state was growing increasingly strong, insomuch as that in the English language of that time defining a person with the term humour meant that the person was perverted or eccentric. The modern meaning of the term comes precisely from this perverted aspect of the ancient meaning. Extravagant people, in fact, were often laughed at, and were also the topic of somebody's jokes. People imitating them were often defined as persons with humour. Due to their ability to make others laugh, the term humour, during the 19th century, assumed the modern meaning, which is typically positive, not negative.

In Europe, the concept of laughter evolved at the same

time as the concept of humour. Before the 18th century, in fact, the act of laughing was considered a negative gesture. At that time, in fact, humour was almost always considered as a way of jeering at somebody, thus as a mockery and a form of aggression, even though not a physical attack. Even Aristotle believed that laughter was a response to other people's deformity or ugliness, though he noted that if the subject provoked other emotions, such as anger, this humorous reaction was not induced. This line of thought endured so much through history that Thomas Hobbes[1], in the 17th century, defined humour as a feeling of superiority, a 'sudden glory', arising from the perception of inferiority of the person being laughed at. More precisely, Hobbes said: 'I may therefore conclude, that the passion of laughter is nothing else but sudden glory arising from some sudden conception of some eminency in ourselves, by comparison with the infirmity of others, or with our own formerly.'

In Europe, in the late 18th century, when the more intellectual side of humour was being emphasized upon, its strong relation to aggressiveness was called into question. Humour began to be seen as the ability to catch the inconsistencies of a situation and thus as a remarkable example of intelligence. Peaceful coexistence and tolerance were new ideals of the modern society brought into light by social shifts, which also triggered this transformation in the vision of humour. It was then that the term humour became free from the negative meaning of the past and the term wit began

---

[1] Thomas Hobbes of Malmesbury (5 April 1588–4 December 1679) was an English philosopher. He was one of the founders of modern political philosophy and political science.

to be used in its place.

Even in India there had been a time when laughing was not very welcome. The following excerpt from Buddhist scriptures gives us the perspective on laughter and humour of an important religious establishment:

> ...At that time, (a) group of 6 monks, laughing a great laugh, went amidst the houses... (to which the Buddha said)... 'Not with loud laughter will I go amidst the houses', is a training to be observed. One should not go amidst the houses with loud laughter. Whoever out of disrespect, laughing a great laugh, goes amidst the houses, there is an offence of wrongdoing, (but) there is no offence if it is unintentional, if he is not thinking, if he does not know, if he is ill, if he only smiles when the matter is one for laughing, if there are accidents, if he is mad, if he is the first wrongdoer.[2]

This regulation comes from the Vinaya, the code of conduct for Buddhist monks and nuns, and is one of over 220 rules for monastic behaviour. For a Buddhist monk in ancient India, to laugh out loud was an offence, a matter requiring confession and expiation in front of the entire assembly of fellow monastics. Ancient Buddhism was opposed to humour and laughter. Later, Buddhist scholastics developed a scheme of 6 kinds of laughter, or perhaps we should rather say of amusement, ranging from 'sita', an almost imperceptible smile manifest in the subtleties of facial expression to 'atihasita', the most boisterous, uproarious laughter attended by movements

---

[2]http://www.academia.edu/801664/Real_Buddhas_dont_laugh_attitudes_towards_humour_and_laughter_in_ancient_India_and_China

of the entire body'. Of these, a Buddhist would be expected to indulge only in the first kind.

It is worth noticing that western scholars have a consistent perception that humour hardly existed in ancient India. There are mainly 2 reasons for this: firstly, much of early Indian humour was scatological and erotic in nature. In the western-language translations erotic passages were (are) either omitted entirely or given only in a heavily Latinized form. This extends even to the names of characters in ancient Indian plays, some of which, if translated literally and presented at certain university campuses today, might give rise to sexual harassment charges. Secondly, we must consider the vagaries of time and history. In the hot, humid climate of most of India, without chemically treated paper, a manuscript might have had a life span of little more than over 50 years before it needed to be rewritten. With few people being literate, only the most important texts would survive, and we can read 'important' as 'serious'. Despite these tendencies to de-humourize Indian texts, a new appreciation of Indian humour has come into being since the publication of Lee Siegel's *Laughing Matters*. In a sense, Siegel argues that all Indian literature is comic. The western idea of literature as bifurcated between tragedy and comedy does not apply to India. In Indian literature, there is always a happy ending for the main protagonists, even if it needs to be postponed by a reincarnation or two.

Defining Humour
(or, at least trying to do so)

Interestingly, a word as frequently used as the word humour has such a multiplicity of meaning that it is difficult to define and interpret it correctly.

Arthur Asa Berger defined humour as, 'A specific type of communication that establishes an incongruent relationship or meaning and is presented in a way that causes laughter.' Hence, he focused his definition of humour on audience's interpretation and response. Charles Winick, instead, focused his attention on the speaker's intention, thus defining a joke as, 'Any type of communication that has a witty or funny intent that is known in advance by the teller.' In Winick's definition, unsuccessful attempts to be humorous can be explained, since it is the intention, and not the response that matters. In some instances, there may be a positive response (laughter) even if the intention of the speaker was not to amuse.

William Martineau tried to find a definition suitable for different cases, thus he underlined that 'humour is conceived generically to be any communicative instance which is perceived as humorous by any of the interacting parties.' This definition, that underlines the final status (every party perceived to be in a humorous situation) rather than the initial one, presents a 'funny' limitation: to define humour he utilizes the term humour itself. His intention to provide a better understanding of the **term seems** to go in the opposite direction, highlighting how **hum**our may be a concept hardly definable, though everyone understands it.

Many people consider the terms humour and joke as interchangeable while others highlight their differences. Debra Long and Arthur Graesser, for example, stated, 'Humour is anything done or said purposefully or inadvertently that is found to be comical or amusing. In contrast, jokes are defined as anything done or said to deliberately provoke amusement.' In other words, to define something as humorous, the reaction of the audience is fundamental while for jokes the intention of the teller is what matters.

Another interesting distinction proposed by Long and Graesser is that it links both the terms to the context: 'Jokes are also context free and self-contained in the sense that they can be told in many conversational contexts. Wit will be defined as anything deliberately said that provokes amusement in a specific conversational context.' Jokes may be transposed and reused more easily in different situations and they may also be more easily understood because they embody in themselves a lot more information compared to humour, that instead is more linked to a specific context or event. Nevertheless, sometimes even jokes require a certain stock of knowledge that may not be shared by everyone. For example, jokes about the Queen Elizabeth in the UK, jokes about attorneys in the

US, or jokes about the Carabinieri (Italian police with military and civil duties) require the audience to be aware of and to comprehend some stereotype connected to these figures.

Therefore, at the end of the story, it seems that humour cannot be precisely defined (or, at least nobody was able to clearly define it) even if everyone understands its meaning.

Why Do We Laugh?

It might be of different frequencies, but everyone laughs and that is for sure. But:

- Why do we laugh?
- What is considered to be amusing?
- Which are the mental processes that enable the appreciation of humour?
- Which are the essential 'ingredients' to obtain a positive response to humour?

As usual, there is no scarcity of theories aimed at providing answers to the above questions and as you can imagine theories concerning humour are in great number. John Young Thomson Greig, back in 1923, created a list of 88 theories! Do not worry; I am not going to list all of them here. To summarize, we can say that there are 5 main theories, to which all the others can be traced back:

- psychoanalytic
- superiority

- arousal
- incongruity
- reversal

Over time, different degrees of emphasis have been placed on each of these theories. One of the main trends is not to seek any all-embracing theories, but to focus the attention on specific but complementary aspects.

Psychoanalytic

The psychoanalytic theory's founder is Sigmund Freud, who approaches the subject in 2 different works: *Jokes and Their Relation to the Unconscious*, 1905, and *Humour*, 1928. Freud asserts that laughter results from the need to release a surplus of nervous energy. According to Freud, there are 3 fundamental categories of phenomena connected to laughter:

- wit and jokes
- humour
- the comic

Each one of them makes use of specific mechanisms to store energy and then disperse it as laughter.

For example, in Freud's view, the reason we laugh at a joke is because it enables the release of sexual and aggressive impulses. In these occasions, we do not feel the natural guilt because our conscience is temporarily beguiled by the cognitive effort of understanding the joke, thus making it difficult to evaluate the aggressive or sexual content of the joke itself. Although Freud acknowledges the existence of jokes lacking one or both the above mentioned elements, but practically he was never able to enumerate either of them!

> ### Psychoanalytic: Happiness
>
> 'For 22 years my husband and I were the happiest people in the world! Then we met.'
>
> According to the psychoanalytic theory, the wife has some tension with her husband (it does not mean that they have serious issues, but it is enough to cause a little bit of stress, even unconsciously) and she releases her stress and aggression by means of a joke.

Laughter resulting from humour, instead, shows itself when a person finds himself/herself in a stressful or unfavourable situation, for which generally he/she would feel angry and/or fear, and the detection of incongruent elements allows him/her to see it from a different perspective. In this instance, thus, laugher comes from the release of energies generally associated with negative feelings, but which in this specific situation, thanks to the change of perspective, can be expressed as laughter of relief. Humour, in this perspective, represents a defence mechanism that allows people to handle difficult and stressful life situations better. Freud even describes this humour as 'the highest of the defence mechanisms'. This self-defence mechanism, differs from the ability to understand jokes, which is very widespread, it does not present itself in every human being. Actually, some individuals are able to see the funny and positive side of a certain situation, while others, even in the same circumstances, react by showing negative feelings.

The last category identified by Freud, the comic, is the only one that relates laughter to non-verbal stimuli, such as, for example, a person slipping on the ice, or a person who is walking while checking a smartphone knocks himself/

herself into a pole. In these situations, a person employs part of their attention to follow the actions of another person through an anticipatory mechanism, and when the action takes an unexpected course compared to the expectation, there is a release of energies—that is not useful anymore—which becomes laughter. Even in this form, though, there is a good amount of aggression because the event that triggers laughter is typically a negative event for the person to whom it occurred.

Freud's humour theory has been tested through several experiments. Nowadays we can conclude that:

- People tend to consider jokes that emphasize aggressive content as less funny.
- The idea that people who usually repress their sexual instincts or aggression, mostly like jokes that contain both these elements, is not supported.
- The hypothesis that stimulating aggression of the sexual sphere causes a higher appreciation of jokes containing these elements, is also not supported.
- Freud's proposed model, which sees laughter as an outpouring for energy in surplus, does not appear to be consistent with the modern discoveries about the functioning of the nervous system.

These are the main reasons for the scientific world's declining interest since the '80s in Freud's theory concerning jokes.

Generally speaking, one of the greatest limitations of Freud's theory is that it does not take into account the social sphere, but only the inner individual dynamics.

Superiority

It is quite evident that a good share of humour is based on some sort of aggressiveness. Aggressiveness may be expressed in several ways, creating juxtaposition between different groups: males and females, young and elderly, blacks and whites etc. There is no necessity for the differences to be sharp in order to bring out the humour of the juxtaposition.

The superiority theory is one of the oldest approaches to humour and it can be dated back to Plato and Aristotle, more than 2,000 years ago. Plato stated that laughter originates in malice; we laugh at what is ridiculous in other people, feeling delight instead of pain when we see others' misfortune. Similarly, Aristotle saw comedy as an imitation of people with characteristics below the average, and thus ill-fated.

As introduced before, even Hobbes upholds this theory and defines laughter as a 'sudden glory', derived from comparing ourselves with someone who in that specific situation presents lower characteristics than ourselves.

One of the most active advocates of the superiority theory is Charles Gruner, who views humour as 'playful aggression', with the word 'play' referring to a competition, a contest. According to Gruner, even the more peaceful forms of humour actually hide some form of superiority and winner/losers logic. For example, the word play itself can be seen as a proof of lexical superiority of the author over the audience. This has led to the creation of a sort of Gruner's rule that shows how in order to understand a piece of humorous material it is necessary only to find out who is ridiculed, how and why. He also adds, 'What is necessary and sufficient to cause laughter is a combination of a loser, a victim of derision or ridicule, with suddenness of loss.'

It does seem according to this approach that there cannot be any self-directed humour, since it is hard to conceive that both the winner and the loser are the same person. Gruner solves this contradiction by arguing that we feel superior over the person we behaved as when the event happened.

Someone can say that the superiority theory describes the human being as baleful and violent, and humour is the tool that legitimizes these characteristics. In actuality, Gruner himself underlines that the aggressiveness that the humour holds can be a form of play, without any real intention to inflict pain to anybody. For example, when a person tells a racist joke, it does not mean he/she is a racist and the same holds true for the people who laugh at that joke. The understanding and amusement do not spring out from the identification with the winner, but more on the knowledge of the stereotype that is the key to the reading of the content.

> **Superiority: Too much swinging**
>
> During a meeting a colleague continued to swivel in his chair. Then, while he was expressing his opinion, the chair slipped and the colleague fell on the ground.
>
> This a typical example of a funny situation where you laugh because you feel superior to your colleague since he fell in a very stupid and childish way.

Following the superiority theory, some may think that the more a joke shows hostility the more amusing it is. Some researchers have sustained this hypothesis, while others show that a content with a moderate level of hostility results in more amusement than one with a low or high level of hostility. Finally, others note that the amusement is derived more from the perceived pain experienced by the 'victim' than from the hostility displayed. Even in this instance, the suffering is not a real one since it is still in a playful context.

Another prediction of superiority theory would seem to be that people who are more hostile will enjoy humour more than the less aggressive people do, since any kind of humour is based on aggressiveness. There has been no evidence supporting this hypothesis, while it has been noted that people who are more aggressive tend to prefer a more hostile kind of humour.

Currently, superiority theory does not have much acceptance, since humour is seen more as having positive connotations, which hardly reconcile themselves with the idea of aggressiveness. In any case, this approach helps introducing the concept that humour serves as a means of defence from stress and protection from adversity. As humour may provide a sense of victory towards the others, it can become a means to boost one's self-esteem and to keep a balance of mind.

Arousal

Daniel Berlyne (1924–76) was interested in psychological aspects of aesthetic experiences in general, including the appreciation of arts and the enjoyment of play, only after he began to study humour. He noticed that there is an inverted-U relationship between psychological arousal and subjective pleasure, which is: up to a certain point the increase of psychological arousal also increases the subjective pleasure, after a certain point the increase of psychological arousal decreases the subjective pleasure. There are 2 arousal-related mechanisms, which he names as 'arousal boost' and 'arousal jag' mechanisms.

Arousal boost operates during the telling of a joke

or perception of a humorous situation. This increases the psychological arousal to a level where it causes pleasure. The arousal jag, instead, takes over when the arousal boost mechanism is so high it has begun to be aversive, and it serves to bring back the arousal level to pleasurable again. Rather than viewing laughter as a method of releasing an excess of arousal, Berlyne sees it as an expression of pleasure resulting from the change in arousal to an optimal level. Though similar processes take place also in the appreciation of arts, humour is distinguished from these other types by the brief timescale on which the arousal changes occur and the extreme bizarreness of the links that bind the components of the humoristic situation, for e.g. wordplays or puns.

Incongruence

Incongruence theory is mostly focused on cognitive aspects, while considering emotional and social aspects as secondary factors. Schopenhauer stated that 'the cause of laughter in every case is simply the sudden perception of incongruity between a concept and the real object which have been thought through it in some relation, and laughter itself is just the expression of this incongruity.'

Put in another way, in the humorous mode of thinking a thing could be both X and non-X at the same time, contrary to the rational logic. Indeed, it is the activation of 2 contradictory perceptions that represents the essence of humour. Although it is worth noting that many humorous situations present some form of aggressiveness, this is not considered as the true source of humour anymore. Incongruity theory by itself is not sufficient, since the oddity of pairing 2 separate events, even during a limited time range, is not enough to make someone laugh (take a car accident as an example. An accident is incongruous with the normal course of action but it is not funny by itself.). For these reasons, the so-called incongruity-resolution theory has been developed, where for the incongruity to be funny, it must also be resolved in a way that makes sense and that does not harm anyone. The mental process thus required to identify the incongruity is to retrace the situation/event in order to identify an alternative solution that makes sense.

Jerry Suls proposed a 2-stage model for humour comprehension. The first stage is called situation set-up, and it causes the listener to make prediction about the likely outcome. When the punchline does not conform to the prediction, the second stage begins, and the listener is surprised and tries to find a cognitive meaning that will make the punchline follow from the material presented in the set-up. When this key to the reading is found, the incongruity is removed and laughter ensues. If a cognitive rule, a key to the reading, is not found, however, the joke cannot be perceived as funny and does not lead to laughter. According to this theory, thus, humour arises from the removal of the incongruity, rather than from its persistence.

Incongruity-Resolution: 2 fishes

2 fishes in a tank. One turns to the other and says: 'Do you know how to drive this?'

The set-up line leads us to think about 2 fishes in a fish tank. But the punchline surprises us: why should the fish be able to drive a fish tank? Then, we suddenly realize that the word 'tank' has 2 meanings, and that the fishes are actually in an army tank.

> **Incongruity: No resolution, not funny**
>
> Let us take the above joke and let us modify it in order to remove the resolution.
>
> 2 fishes in an army tank. One turns to the other and says: 'Do you know how to drive this?'
>
> In this case, there is still an incongruity: why 2 fishes should be in an army tank? However, there is no resolution.
>
> P.S. If you find this joke funny too, please visit a doctor.

One may think that the harder it is to predict the punchline of a joke, the funnier is the joke. However, it has been noticed that the funniest jokes are those where listeners can 'see the punchline coming' and not the ones that are completely unexpected. It can be concluded that laughter is a partial exclamation of achievement rather than an expression of surprise over incongruity.

Reversal

If you found the information so far strange or you are not satisfied with the above mentioned theories that explain why we laugh, you are right. In fact, the large majority of researches study the mechanisms of humour, but do not take into consideration the context in which it is created and spent, which is not regarded as important enough but as a playful situation. Max Eastman (1883–1969) stated: 'no definition of humour, no theory of wit, no explanation of comic laughter, will ever stand up, which is not based upon the distinction between playful and serious.'

The concept of humour as a play is promoted by Michael Apter through a more extensive theory about motivation and personality called reversal theory. According to Apter, humour exists only if our mind is set into 'play mode', which allows us to have 'protection zones' created in order to isolate ourselves from the real and serious problems of the world.

Apter has called this mental play mode 'paratelic', in contrast with the other mental status called 'telic' that represents the more serious mode. Apter states that on a regular day everyone changes his/her status from telic to paratelic several times, which is why it is known as the reversal theory.

When in telic state, one is very focused on one's goal and less on the ways to achieve it, whereas in paratelic state the focus is on the activities that lead to the goal and which are experienced with a less tension. Apter underlines how the arousal is experienced differently depending on the mental state in which one is. For example, an arousal can cause anxiety when experienced in telic state, but it can bring joy and excitement if experienced when in paratelic mode. Therefore, the reasons are clear for why certain topics can be experienced positively or negatively depending on the context shared by listeners and also the prevalent mind frame.

Humour Theories at Work: The Slippery Floor

Let's consider a typical scene seen in many films and in real life: falling on a slippery floor (it can be because of ice, oil, water, a banana peel etc.), and let's apply the different theories we have seen so far.

According to the psychoanalytical theory, this is related to the comic category and we laugh because the course of action follows an unexpected path and the act of falling permits the release of the energy that is not useful for people anymore.

According to the superiority theory, we laugh because in

the moment the person falls, we feel superior to him/her. It can be noticed that if from an emotional perspective we do not like the person who falls (imagine a good-looking person that walk in a very pretentious way, in an attempt to act like a top model), we will laugh more compared to if a person we like falls. This is because in that moment we feel superior to a person who tried, thanks to his/her behaviour, to be superior to us.

If we use the arousal theory, we can say that if a very old person falls on a slippery floor (or a person with mobility issues), we are not likely to laugh because the arousal would have passed the optimum level, since we would feel more scared for the consequences of the fall than the pleasure to see something unexpected.

The incongruity theory will explain the act of falling as not congruous with the normal setting, which is just walking along the corridor, street etc. Normally, if along with the person who falls his/her personal belongings also 'fly away', we laugh more because the situation is then more incongruous with the normal path. However, also the resolution plays a role. In case the person did not report any injury, ideally we continue laughing, but if the person is suffering then we stop laughing. Again, in the case of an old person falling, we probably do not laugh at all since the resolution does not elicit acceptable emotions.

Finally, using the reversal theory, if we are in a telic mode (for example, involved in a serious conversation), we are probably not going to laugh but if we are having a good time with our friends (that is, we are in paratelic mode), laugh may occur.

Individual Differences in Humour

Everyone has experienced situations in which a joke or any other source of humour was understood by someone and not understood or even disliked by someone else.

That means that people have different humour styles and they perceive humour in different ways. Unfortunately, it seems that universal humour does not exist even if recently some authors have tried to demonstrate the opposite.

Apart from individual differences coming from strictly personal experiences, it has been noted that some differences can be explained by taking into consideration variables such as age, gender and culture.

Here is a brief explanation of how those variables shape the way we use and appreciate humour.

Humour and Age

We know a lot about humour in children, but there is a scarcity of knowledge related to humour throughout other stages of life as well as on understanding if and how humour changes with age is very rare.

Willibald Ruch, Renè Proyer and Marco Weber took a large survey (of almost 43,000 people!) on humour as a sign of character strength. The results showed that humour decreases until the age of 50, and that in men it tends to increase again between the ages of 51 to 62 years.

Willibald Ruch, Paul McGhee and Franz-Joseph Hehl collected survey results from over 4,000 individuals of German nationality, ranging from 14 to 66 years old. 20 different jokes and cartoons were evaluated on their funny and aversive quotient. It emerged that incongruity resolution humour increased in funniness, whereas nonsense humour decreased in funniness among progressively older subjects after the late teens. The degree of aversiveness of both forms of humour generally decreased over the ages sampled.

In a research conducted in a work setting of over 290 workers, Wayne Decker studied how job satisfaction related to age, gender, sense of humour of the supervisor, and the use of sexual humour by the supervisor. In general, the differences between ratings given to supervisors with a low or high sense of humour were greater for younger (under 15) subjects than older ones. Older females downgraded supervisors who used sexual humour, while younger females and males did not.

Rod Martin et al. administered the Humour Styles Questionnaire[3] to more than 1,000 subjects ranging in age from 14 to 87 years old; they found out that elderly individuals scored lower than young people both in affiliative humour and aggressive humour. Moreover, elderly women scored higher

---

[3] The Humour Styles Questionnaire (HSQ) was developed by Rod Martin and Patricia Doris (2003) to measure individual differences in styles of humour.

than the younger ones in self-enriching humour, indicating thus a more humorous vision of life and the use of humour as a tool for coping. There was no significant difference in the use of self-defeating humour.

Jennifer Stanley and some other researchers had 30 young adults, 22 middle-aged people, and 29 senior citizens watch a variety of different sitcom clips. The subjects rated how socially appropriate and funny they found each clip. Stanley also used facial electromyography to determine how much the clips caused their facial muscles to move to form a smile. Moreover, for the record, 'to be coded as a smile, there had to be an upturn of the corners of the lips, plus a wrinkling of the crow's feet at the corners of the eyes, or a pushing up of the cheeks.' What the authors found was that senior citizens were much less likely to be fans of the aggressive style of humour. The 64 to 84-year-olds found a specific clip about 23 per cent less funny than the middle-aged people did, and about 19 per cent less funny than the 17 to 21-year-olds did.

Young adults were also more likely to smirk at the clips that showed self-deprecating humour. The older participants, meanwhile, liked affiliative humour—the kind of jokes that bring people together through a funny or awkward situation.

Stanley suspects a big reason for the generation gap in humour is that as we age, we experience a variety of physical and emotional setbacks—declining cognitive faculties, friends who pass away—and the affiliative style of humour helps us deal with these losses.

Prathiba Shammi and Donald Stuss carried out a study with 2 different age groups—the average ages being 73 and 29; they presented the groups with a test requiring completing a joke with one of the options provided. They noticed that the older age group made more mistakes when selecting the punchline, while the 2 groups do not show any difference when asked to perform a similar test on non-humorous material. They also noticed that the older participants appreciated humoristic material more than the younger ones.

Aron Schaier and Victor Cirelli studied 96 participants divided into 3 age groups—50–59, 60–69, 70–79. All the groups were presented with 12 conservation jokes (based on the concepts of conservation of mass, weight, and volume for their comprehension) and 12 non-conservation jokes. Researchers noticed that for both types of jokes the appreciation deepens with the increasing age of the participant, while understanding decreases.

I do not want to be impolite but it seems that old people laugh more than young people do, but they also do not fully understand the reason for laughing more.

Summary of humour and age

- The more you age, the less you appreciate nonsense, aversive and aggressive humour.
- The more you age, the more you appreciate incongruity-resolution humour.
- The more females age, the less they appreciate sexual humour (at least the one of their boss).
- The more females age, the more they use self-enriching humour.
- It seems (but it is not very sure) that the more you age, the more you appreciate affiliative humour.
- The more you age, the more you appreciate humour but unfortunately it seems that you also understand it less.

Humour and Gender

The role of women in the humour field follows the evolution that women have gone through in the business world. Traditionally, it has been pointed out that women do not tell jokes. Freud asserted that women did not need a sense of humour since they already had many repressed feelings to manage!

Freud was not the only person that had a 'peculiar' consideration of a woman's sense of humour. Robin Lakoff had a very distinct position on this regard: in a study on comprehending jokes, he even stated that women did not have a sense of humour!

Fortunately, someone else claimed that women did not tell jokes very frequently because they had a different communication style, a less aggressive one, and that men and women have different perceptions of the world and thus they may also have different interests and preferences of what humour concerns.

Only later it was noticed that women indeed participated in humoristic activities, but mostly as humour appreciators, rather than humour initiators. Martin Lambert and Susan Ervin-Tripp supported that: 'When it comes to humour, men are more likely to joke, tease, and kid, whereas women are more likely to act as an appreciative audience than to produce humour on their own.' We have also to underline that still many societies are such that women have to work within the social symbols of the dominant group, so it is more likely that women will recognize the joking interests of males than vice-versa. This vision causes asymmetries in the perception of the role of women in humour, insomuch as Mercilee Jenkins reported: 'I wondered why it was that when a man tells a joke and women don't laugh, we are told we have no sense of humour, but when a woman tells a joke and men don't laugh, we are told we are not funny.' However, it is clear that the focus on the understanding or on the telling of a joke is not representative of the world of humour since the vast majority of humour is spontaneous and situation-dependent.

In the light of the superiority theory, some people saw humour as a display of power, which in work setting was typically associated with masculine figures. It was therefore unacceptable for women to display humour in mixed gender groups. Leigh Marlowe observes: 'When women produce and present humour they reverse conventional social situations by putting themselves in the foreground, threatening the most basic social gender arrangements.'

Judging the humour of women in mixed gender contexts can be misleading. Unfortunately, many studies on humour have made this mistake. For example, many of them were focused on the public sphere, which is easier to study compared to private settings, but which also traditionally saw men as the dominant characters, and where women's humour may be distorted by these social relations. In addition, many researches were conducted in laboratories, and asked people to judge cartoon humour and jokes which are, in the real world, a minor source of humour.

I do not want to bore you with research methodology but one study deserves your attention in order to understand how easy it is to jump to the wrong conclusion if you use the wrong approach. Joe Cox et al. studied humour in work settings. They created a questionnaire of 15 hypothetical situations where a colleague was faced with a potentially embarrassing situation. For each situation, there were three possible reactions:

ignoring, helping or reacting with humour. For each of these alternatives respondents should pass judgement on the level of their agreement with that specific reaction. The main issue with this study was that in case a respondent did not choose the humour option he/she was indicated as having little sense of humour. In actuality, because of how the study was designed, researchers were measuring if the respondent appreciated that specific kind of humour, especially disparaging humour, not their sense of humour in general. If men and women would have been presented with different types of humour, these experiments would have led to erroneous conclusions, as it happened. Men, as a matter of fact, assigned higher assessments to the options considered to be humorous, while women preferred to react with helping actions. Cox et al. thus concluded that: 'This study seems to verify what most of the non-empirical literature has hypothesized about women's use of humour, namely, that humour is less a part of the female's communications pattern.' If you disagree with this conclusion, I agree with you.

Mary Crawford and Diane Gressley also used a questionnaire asking participants to indicate someone they knew, who has a particularly effective sense of humour. Results were interesting: the 92 women participating in the research indicated 62 men as individuals with excellent sense of humour, while the 49 men participating indicated the other 41 men as having excellent sense of humour. Researchers noticed that men preferred a more aggressive type of humour and they used jokes more frequently, while women preferred 'slice of life' stories. Aside from these differences, it followed that humour preferences were very similar.

Susan Ervin-Tripp and Martin Lampert noticed that men

were more inclined to start humorous situations, while women tended to keep the humorous situation going, widening it to the other people there. Hence, they noted a sort of collaborative humour, as well as a greater use of puns. Ultimately, humour aimed at oneself was often used as a reaction to other people's humour, but men started it of their own free will to use it against themselves, generally in a more exaggerated and clearly false way.

Traditionally, men were thought to appreciate sexual humour more than women did, but this was true only for what concerned sexual jokes presenting sexist content, which typically have women as targets for the jokes. It has been noted that sexual jokes with no sexist contents do not show significant differences between men and women. Despite the aggressive and sexual kind of humour being generally associated with men only, it has also been found with similar frequency in the women's world as well but only in instances where all members of a group were women. Therefore, if you are a man and you are scared about what kind of jokes your wife or girlfriend is going to tell about you to her female friends, you are simply right!

Summary of humour and gender

- In the past it was believed that women had no sense of humour!
- Many studies related to humour and women were simply wrong.
- Women are less humour initiators compared to men but once humour starts they try to keep it alive.
- Women are less likely to tell jokes, they prefer conversational humour.

- Women do not like aggressive humour very much, they prefer 'slice of life' stories.
- Traditionally, sexual humour was associated only with men. But if you ever listen to a women-only group, you will change your mind!

Humour Styles

With regard to the several categorizations of humour styles that have been proposed, the classification suggested by Rod Martin et al. is one of the most recurrent and relevant ones in the management literature. According to this categorization, there are 4 main humour styles:

- affiliative
- self-enhancing
- aggressive
- self-defeating

These humour styles are the result of the possible combinations of 2 main dimensions: the humour initiator's intention (benevolent vs detrimental) and the focus (self vs relationship). Affiliative and self-enhancing kinds of humour are often defined as positive humour styles, while aggressive and self-defeating humour usually have negative connotations.

Affiliative humour is a humour style that encourages interpersonal interactions and nurtures a positive working environment. Individuals who employ an affiliative style of humour have the tendency to tell jokes and funny stories, amuse others and enjoy laughing along with them. They are usually liked and seen as non-threatening by others, since they use humour as a way to attract people and enhance social interactions. Within an organizational context, indeed, affiliative humour helps to reduce interpersonal tensions and build relationships, enhance group cohesiveness and promote creativity. At individual level, affiliative humour contributes to increased self-esteem, mental equilibrium, social intimacy, psychological well-being, extraversion and openness; while reducing stress and anxiety.

Self-enhancing humour is generally used as a coping mechanism to reduce the negative impact of a stressful situation and keep a positive attitude towards it. People who employ a self-enhancing style of humour show a witty approach to life and are not excessively concerned by its unavoidable troubles. In an organizational setting, self-enhancing humour can be used to improve one's own image before others, encourage creativity and reduce stress. Indeed, from a psychological perspective, this humour style is negatively associated with neuroticism and anxiety, while it has a positive correlation with self-esteem, extroversion and openness, similar to affiliative humour. Compared to the latter, however, self-enhancing humour has a more egocentric connotation.

Aggressive humour is the kind used to disparage, put down, or manipulate others and the use of ridicule, offensive humour and compulsive expression of humour even when it is inappropriate. Aggressive humour is used to victimize, deride and provoke other kinds of disparagement towards the focus of the humorous expression, and people who use this style often aim to influence others through an implicit threat of derision. It is usually adopted to insult or humiliate other people, in order to increase their anxiety and reduce their well-being. In an organizational setting, aggressive humour may be used especially by higher-level members to underline their rank or status towards lower-level employees. From a psychological perspective, aggressive humour is negatively related to friendliness and relationship satisfaction, while it is positively associated with neuroticism.

Self-defeating humour is used by individuals who have a tendency to ridicule themselves, usually in order to make others laugh or to be liked by being the butt of their jokes. In an organizational context, individuals who use this style quite frequently may do it to reduce their status and make themselves closer to lower-level employees, or to feel more accepted by others. Self-defeating and affiliative humour are similar in the way how they both improve relationships, but they differ because the former is used at the initiator's expense. This humour style is often seen as a defence mechanism to deal with negative self-esteem, and individuals who employ it are used to report higher levels of anxiety and neuroticism, and lower levels of agreeableness, conscientiousness, intimacy and psychological well-being.

Humour styles in practice

Setting: A company is spread out on 5 different floors of a building. There are 2 elevators. They are quite slow and not very reliable. At least twice every month someone gets stuck in between 2 floors, requesting the support of the maintenance department to exit it. Each elevator can carry up to 4 people (320 kg). On the right side of the elevators is the staircase.

2 colleagues are waiting for the elevator to get to their office. One of the colleagues is carrying 2 books in one hand and 3 snacks on the other. This colleague is also overweight.

Affiliative Humour

One colleague, noticing the one with books and snacks: 'Food for your thoughts?' The other, while smiling, replied: 'No, it is just the survival kit for the elevator!'

In this case, you can see that humour is not against anyone. It is just a way to create a bond between colleagues and not to be bored while waiting for the elevator.

Self-enhancing Humour

A third colleague passes behind the other two in order to take the staircase. They know each other for over 10 years and they are have a good relationship. One of the colleagues says: 'The elevator is coming, would you like to ride it?' He replied, while smiling: 'No thanks, I can go faster than that elevator by jumping on even a single leg!'

You can see in this example that the humorous reply is able to generate a moderate smile, not a loud laugh. It is not a rule, but very often self-enhancing humour is not the most powerful one.

Aggressive Humour

One of the colleagues: 'The elevator is coming, would you like to ride it?' He replied, while smiling: 'No thanks, I guess the elevator already has a lot of work with you two!' They replied with a smile.

In this case, it is clear that the colleague is underlining the fact that one of the other colleagues is overweight. He said it with a smile, probably because of the good relationship that he shared with the other two. But surely his reply was not considered very funny by the others and even if they replied with a smile, (probably a fake one) in their minds they probably thought: 'I hope a car hits you while crossing the street!'

Self-defeating Humour

In this case, the third colleague is quite overweight himself. The other two are the same as before. One of the colleagues: 'The elevator is coming, would you like a ride?' He replied, while smiling: 'No thanks, I do not want to be remembered as the person who made an attempt on the lives of his colleagues!'

In this case, it is clear that the person is joking about his own physical condition.

Finding Your Humour Style: Humour Style Questionnaire

Professor Rod Turner has gently permitted me to use his famous Humour Style Questionnaire (HSQ)[4], probably the best of its kind.

Beginning of the Questionnaire

People experience and express humour in many different

---

[4] Martin, R.A.; Puhlik-Doris, P.; Larsen G.; Gray, J. & Weir, K. (2003), 'Individual Differences in Uses of Humor and Their Relation to Psychological Well-being: Development of the Humor Styles Questionnaire', *Journal of Research in Personality*, 37, 48–75.

ways. Below is a list of statements describing the different ways in which humour might be experienced. Please read each statement carefully, and indicate the degree to which you agree or disagree with it. Please respond as honestly and objectively as you can. Use the following scale:

Totally disagree	Moderately disagree	Slightly disagree	Neither agree nor disagree	Slightly agree	Moderately agree	Totally agree
1	2	3	4	5	6	7

1.	I usually don't laugh or joke around much with other people.	1	2	3	4	5	6	7
2.	If I am feeling depressed, I can usually cheer myself up with humour.	1	2	3	4	5	6	7
3.	If someone makes a mistake, I often tease them about it.	1	2	3	4	5	6	7
4.	I let people laugh at me or make fun at my expense more than I should.	1	2	3	4	5	6	7
5.	I don't have to work very hard at making other people laugh—I seem to be a naturally humorous person.	1	2	3	4	5	6	7
6.	Even when I'm by myself, I'm often amused by the absurdities of life.	1	2	3	4	5	6	7
7.	People are never offended or hurt by my sense of humour.	1	2	3	4	5	6	7
8.	I often get carried away in putting myself down if it makes my family or friends laugh.	1	2	3	4	5	6	7
9.	I rarely make other people laugh by telling funny stories about myself.	1	2	3	4	5	6	7

10.	If I am feeling upset or unhappy I usually try to think of something funny about the situation to make myself feel better.	1	2	3	4	5	6	7
11.	When telling jokes or saying funny things, I am usually not very concerned about how other people are taking it.	1	2	3	4	5	6	7
12.	I often try to make people like or accept me more by saying something funny about my own weaknesses, blunders, or faults.	1	2	3	4	5	6	7
13.	I laugh and joke a lot with my friends.	1	2	3	4	5	6	7
14.	My humorous outlook on life keeps me from getting overly upset or depressed about things.	1	2	3	4	5	6	7
15.	I do not like it when people use humour as a way of criticizing or putting someone down.	1	2	3	4	5	6	7
16.	I don't often say funny things to put myself down.	1	2	3	4	5	6	7
17.	I usually don't like to tell jokes or amuse people.	1	2	3	4	5	6	7
18.	If I'm by myself and I'm feeling unhappy, I make an effort to think of something funny to cheer myself up.	1	2	3	4	5	6	7
19.	Sometimes I think of something that is so funny that I can't stop myself from saying it, even if it is not appropriate for the situation.	1	2	3	4	5	6	7
20.	I often go overboard in putting myself down when I am making jokes or trying to be funny.	1	2	3	4	5	6	7

21.	I enjoy making people laugh.	1	2	3	4	5	6	7
22.	If I am feeling sad or upset, I usually lose my sense of humour.	1	2	3	4	5	6	7
23.	I never participate in laughing at others even if all my friends are doing it.	1	2	3	4	5	6	7
24.	When I am with friends or family, I often seem to be the one that other people make fun of or joke about.	1	2	3	4	5	6	7
25.	I don't often joke around with my friends.	1	2	3	4	5	6	7
26.	It is my experience that thinking about some amusing aspect of a situation is often a very effective way of coping with problems.	1	2	3	4	5	6	7
27.	If I don't like someone, I often use humour or teasing to put them down.	1	2	3	4	5	6	7
28.	If I am having problems or feeling unhappy, I often cover it up by joking around, so that even my closest friends don't know how I really feel.	1	2	3	4	5	6	7
29.	I usually can't think of witty things to say when I'm with other people.	1	2	3	4	5	6	7
30.	I don't need to be with other people to feel amused—I can usually find things to laugh about even when I'm by myself.	1	2	3	4	5	6	7
31.	Even if something is really funny to me, I will not laugh or joke about it if someone will be offended.	1	2	3	4	5	6	7
32	Letting others laugh at me is my way of keeping my friends and family in good spirits.	1	2	3	4	5	6	7

How to Calculate Your Score

Affiliative Humour: 1*+ 5+ 9*+ 13+ 17*+ 21+ 25*+ 29*
Self-Enhancing Humour: 2+ 6+ 10+ 14+ 18+ 22*+ 26+ 30
Aggressive Humour: 3+ 7*+ 11+ 15*+ 19+ 23*+ 27+ 31*
Self-defeating Humour: 4+ 8+ 12+ 16*+ 20+ 24+ 28+ 32

Note: Items marked with * are reverse keyed, that is, 1=7, 2=6, 3=5, 4=4, 5=3, 6=2, 7=1. After reversing these items, sum up all 8 items in each scale to obtain scale totals.

Humour in India

As it is in every country, humour in India evolved, is evolving and will continue to evolve. India experimented with some control on humour during the British period, especially with humour on stage and on screen. This has also partially affected humour in private settings and the type of humour that is socially tolerated. During an interview[5], Ashok Chakradhar, a respected poet and comic, described the evolution of humour in India through the evolution of the relationship between men and women: 'In the 1980s, women told men, love me but do not touch me. In the 1990s, they said touch me but do not kiss me. In 1995, they said kiss me but nothing more. In 2000, they said do whatever you want but do not tell anybody. In 2010, they said do something otherwise I will tell everybody you do not know how to do anything. Just as the display of affection has shifted from puritanical restrain to public display, humour is becoming freer and more

---

[5]Vikas Bajaj, 'Humour Comes of Age in India', Published on Indian Ink, *The New York Times*, 27 September 2011.

adventurous in India.'

Humour is important for Indians. On a scale of 1 to 10, for Indian men humour scores 7.95 while for women it is 7.70, not a big difference. When it comes to evaluating the quality of their own humour, men are much more confident than women. In fact, men rate themselves 7.05 while women give only 5.88. But, I am sure you have many personal examples that contradict this result.

As already mentioned, humour may also have negative outcomes. Below are reported those kinds of humour that are not liked by Indians.

Types of Humour Disliked

Type	Percentage
Hurtful	24%
Lame jokes	22%
Embarrassing	11%
Offending	11%
Inappropriate situation	9%
Crosses the line	7%
Misunderstandings	4%
Racism	3%
Inappropriate timing	2%
Sex-related jokes	2%

Source: Hiranandani, 2010

By using the classification of humour that we have already explained (affiliative, self-enhancing, aggressive and self-defeating), it emerges that Indians use the affiliative and self-enhancing humour styles more than the aggressive and self-defeating styles of humour, indicating that they use adaptive humour more than the maladaptive kind. In this case, there is no difference between men and women.[6]

Kinds of Humour Used by Indians

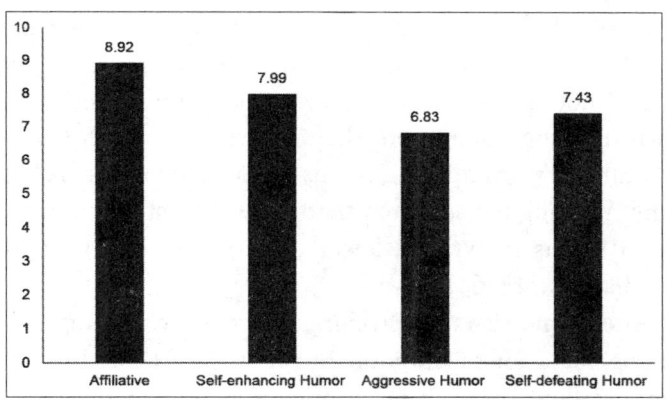

Source: Hiranandani, 2010

As an external observer of Indians and Indian humour, I found it unbelievable (given the geographical distance between the 2 countries) that there were similarities between Indian and Italian humour. When I teach or hold conferences, I usually use a good deal of humour, but while working in international settings I realized that sometimes my humour did not work

---

[6]This was found in a study carried out by N.A. Hiranandani, in which he took into consideration university students who usually have a more aggressive humour style compared to relatively seasoned people. We can thus infer that Indians mostly have a positive humour style.

properly. For this reason, I was apprehensive about my first teaching experience in India. If my humour did not work, I would have to revert to a very serious teaching style which is not really my style.

On my first day of teaching in India, I began the lesson at 9.30 a.m. Within a few minutes my Indian students began laughing (I sincerely hope they were laughing with me and not at me). In my perspective, the first 90 minutes were great. During the break, when students were having fun and joking about, I noticed that their humour was funny to me as well. Before the course finished, they invited me over for dinner and damn, I realized that Indians in social contexts are really funny. We laughed so much that the waiter of the restaurant had to tell us to try and lower the volume of our laughter (not that it worked, but still).

After some years of travelling to India, I can confirm that Indians use a lot of humour. But how do I describe Indian humour? First of all, it very much depends on the context, that is, it is mainly based on the content of a conversation or on a specific situation. Secondly, it is usually not aggressive. This does not mean that humour is never directed against another person, but when it does, it results in increasing social bonds rather than separating people. Thirdly, mostly it is quite polite. While both sexual humour and humour that leverages swear words do exist, its usage is less frequent as compared to other countries—for example Italy, France and USA. Fourthly, it is 'portable'; while there are occasions where in order to understand humour it is necessary to have knowledge of the local culture (films, religions, politicians, cities, etc.), on an average the frequency of culture specific humour in India is quite low so everyone can be engaged in humorous exchanges.

Are Workplaces Funny Places? Are They Looking for Humour?

If one thinks that companies must be the funniest place on Earth, then maybe he/she has the wrong ideas. In my perspective, humour should be enough to create a pleasant working environment, and to support the company's goal. Humour as an autonomous and independent goal can be just detrimental for a company (for example, working for my company was really funny, unfortunately, the company went in bankruptcy because all the people where just laughing together).

On an average, things are more serious inside companies compared to our lives outside of them. It has been observed that people laugh much less during working days compared to non-working ones. Again, this is not a bad thing, it is just normal. On our non-working days we have more spare time (and our boss is not looking at us), but while we work we have to dedicate our attention to the tasks at hand.

The problem is: sometimes managers, colleagues, suppliers, customers think that humour should be not part of the life of the companies because it is considered a waste of time or as something not aligned with business. As a result, business environments are sometimes too serious. Two researchers, Louis Franzini and Susan Haggerty, asked people where they would like to add humour in their lives and an overwhelming response was—work, the most frequent single category mentioned.

In one study of more than 2,500 employees, 81 per cent said they believe a fun working environment would make them more productive. Even more surprising is that 55 per cent said they would take less pay to have more fun at work.

A quite detailed study about the perception and use of humour at the workplace has been carried out by David Autissier and Èlodie Arnéguy. In it emerged that 63 per cent of the employees think that humour is not leveraged enough at the workplace.

It is very important to notice that the above-mentioned results vary greatly depending on the work experience of respondents. It seems that the more people are experienced, the more they desire humour at the workplace. Maybe the explanation is that when people have just joined an organization, they are more focused on showing their commitment and pursuing a good career. As more time passes, people begin noticing other variables too and maybe they feel less pressure in showing that they are good enough for the employer.

It also emerges that humour at the workplace is normally used without specific purpose, it is just part of managing the normal relationships among co-workers. It is also very common to use humour as an ice-breaking aid and to include other people in a discussion or situation. It is interesting to note the frequency of humour used to overcome a taboo, in fact, humour can be used to convey messages in a way that otherwise could be potentially offending or not allowed.

Occasions of Use of Humour at the Workplace

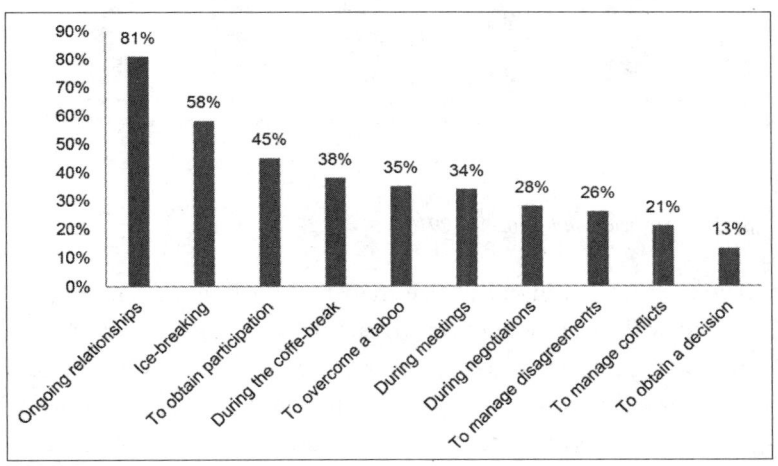

Source: Autissier and Arnéguy, 2010

Fully aligned with the previous data are the results related to the positive outcomes of humour at the workplace. In fact, the most common answer is that humour does not have a specific outcome but it simply improves our lives.

Positive Outcomes of Humour at the Workplace

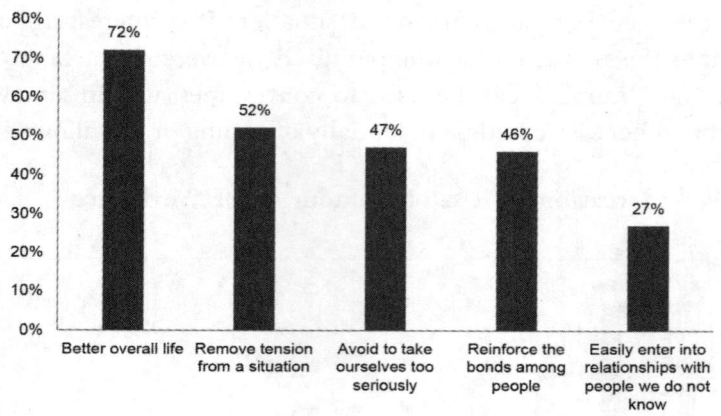

Source: Autissier and Arnéguy, 2010

It is very interesting to notice that the best kind of humour is shared with peers while the worst with superiors. In addition, nearly 1 person out of 4 reports that he/she never shared humour with his/her superior. I might add that this is really bad.

In a survey developed by Accountemps, a specialized staffing service for temporary accounting, finance and bookkeeping professionals, more than 1,400 Chief Financial Officers had been interviewed. They were asked that how important an employee's sense of humour is in him/her fitting into their company's corporate culture. Here are their responses:

- Very important for 22 per cent
- Somewhat important for 57 per cent
- Not at all important for 20 per cent

- Don't know/no answer for 1 per cent

Max Messmer, chairman of Accountemps said: 'Job candidates should let their personality shine when meeting prospective employers. The interview is no place for a stand-up comedy routine, but it is the right time to show hiring managers you are approachable and will be easy to work with.'

I believe humour gets people to actually listen to the speaker either in a meeting, presentation or a learning session. A lot of times it helps people to connect and aids in building trust among colleagues and is a great tool to motivate and engage employees. A leader who uses humour effectively will be able to drive goals, targets leading to increase in productivity.

Bidisha Banerjee,
Chief Talent Development, People Office
Future Group

In another survey of business executives and deans of business schools, 62 per cent of the deans responding to the survey said they felt that humour contributed to executive success; and nearly all the CEOs who responded felt that humour has an important role to play in the conduct of business, and that it helps keep business healthy. The individual conducting the survey noted that nearly all the responding CEOs said that '… all other things being equal, they would hire the job applicant with a better sense of humour.'

> *Humour in workplace is natural since it is a part of human relationships. Helps teams bond, helps relationship between peers, between managers and his subordinates. Humour contributes to healthy relationships. Healthy relationships result in speed of work completion and resilience in the team. Generic taboos are that it should not be personal, but otherwise lines get drawn in an evolving sort of way among the team members.*
>
> *Kaushik Mukherjee*
> *Co-owner*
> *VFS Systems and Services*

Herb Kelleher, co-founder, former CEO and now Chairman Emeritus of Southwest Airlines, is probably the best-known example of a top manager who insists on hiring employees with a good sense of humour. According to Kelleher, in filling any position—'What we are looking for, first and foremost, is a sense of humour… We don't care much about education and expertise, because we can train people… We hire attitudes.' In fact, during job interviews, job candidates are specifically asked to give an example of how they have recently used their sense of humour on the job, and how they have used humour to defuse a difficult situation.

Even NASA has publicly stated that when the space agency recruits future astronauts one of the personality traits they look for is humour, believing that candidates who demonstrate a sense of humour are more flexible, more creative and better able to deal with stress. (Of course, if you are flying to Mars for 17 years with only one other crew member to keep you company, a good sense of humour might just be a lifesaver.)

Organizational Culture and Humour

The concept of corporate or organizational culture refers to the sense of shared values, norms, and behaviour patterns that bind members of an organization together and give it a distinctive identity.

Corporate culture is an important factor in determining the ability of the organization to remain productive and competitive. Part of what makes for a successful organizational culture is a sense of camaraderie shared by the employees and them feeling good about what they do. Humour is a significant ingredient of an organizational culture that is able to create a more positive working environment and to reveal insights and social patterns of any organization.

According to Yiannis Gabriel, Stephen Fineman and David Sims: 'To regard humour and jokes as a superficial phenomenon of organizational life, as has been the custom, misses the rich undercurrent of meanings present. Jokes that people tell at the workplace can reveal as much or perhaps more about the organization, its management, its culture and its conflicts than answers to carefully administered surveys.'

Karen Vinton conducted an observational study on the cultural system of a small, family-owned corporation. In her research, she found that humour reflected the general features of the company's culture and could provide an understanding of other cultural issues such as socialization. In particular, she found that 3 types of humour were signalling a specific cultural insight. First, members of the company enjoying self-ridiculing jokes were communicating their willingness to participate in teasing, and therefore, friendly relationships. In turn, teasing was found to be used especially by senior members of the company as a nice approach to get the work done by junior employees. Finally, bantering behaviours were adopted to reduce status differentials existing among employees and make cooperation and task accomplishment easier.

Humour in workplace is a very valuable ingredient for a successful company with a positive work environment. Without it, the stress levels in modern corporate environment can take a toll on the workplace resulting in poor delivery resulting in lower net income. There has to be some boundary lines that are adhered to in the culture. Employees should not feel targeted and uncomfortable.

Dr Rajkumar Palanna
CFO
eMpulse Global

Many researchers have also found evidence that humour is positively associated with better performances—a hypothesis that finds evidence in organizations such as Southwest Airlines, which are well known for their humour-oriented culture as well as their profitability and growth. Managers should try to include humour in the organizational culture as it represents a great tool to communicate values and norms, accepted and undesirable behaviours. For example, an anecdote mocking someone for engaging in a specific behaviour may be used to signal that behaviour as improper, a method which is particularly useful to strengthen norms or draw attention towards undesired conducts. In particular, affiliative and self-enhancing kinds humour seem to positively contribute in influencing individuals to engage in culture-oriented behaviour.

Patterns of Humour at the Workplace

Humour at the workplace follows some usual patterns depending on the characteristics of the actors involved in the humorous situations.

Craig Lundberg illustrated how person-focused joking in such diverse settings as an electric motor repair shop and an oil exploration party on the north slope of Alaska, both reflected the social rankings in the groups. Meaning, jokes, and especially aggressive ones, tend to start from people ranked socially higher to the ones ranked socially lower.

Janet Holmes and Meredith Marra studied some blue-collar employees in a fairly cohesive and mutually dependent factory work team. They noticed that the employees tended to produce high-frequency humour in the form of brief single quips using a competitive humour style (i.e. trying to outdo the others in witness), but in a socially supportive manner (i.e. using humour to agree with, add to, elaborate, or strengthen the argument of a previous speaker).

On the other hand, during meetings with white-collar staff in a private commercial organization, Holmes and Marra found that there was a good deal of humour also, but it took the form of a more extended, somewhat competitive humour sequences, and tended to be much more contested than supportive (i.e. using humour to challenge, disagree with, or undermine the authority of previous speakers), reflecting the individualistic and competitive culture of that private business.

Another pattern of humour was observed by Holmes and Marra during staff meetings in government departments and non-profit organizations, where humour took the form of extended sequences, a collaborative humour style (i.e. building on and extending one another's humorous comments rather than trying to outdo one another with humour), and a more supportive than contested use of humour, reflecting a generally collegial, focused and cooperative style of interaction in these organizations as a whole.

Jack Duncan and Philip Feisal collected data for 5 years on humour at work from people divided into 25 work groups. Each participant received, together with other general instructions, a list of members in his or her group; a number was assigned to each member. Using these numbers to represent the members, respondents were asked to rate the members of their group on a series of social network issues. An example of such a request was: 'Please list the 3 members of your group you most prefer as friends.' Respondents referred to the numbers assigned to group members and placed the corresponding numbers in the 3 spaces provided in the questionnaire.

Group members were also asked to select their favourite and least favourite leaders and followers, and to identify the best employees in their groups. Questions were also based on the humour network of the group. Such questions included:

'Which 3 members of your group are most (and least) likely to initiate jokes about other people?' and 'Which members of your group are most (and least) likely to be the butt of a joke at work?'

The respondents' social network choices and descriptions of joking patterns revealed four stereotypical over-chosen and over-rejected group members. Two of those were managerial type and other two were non-managerial type. Below is a brief description of each.

The Arrogant Executive

The arrogant executive holds a position of formal authority in the organization but he/she is socially isolated as a result of his or her personal choice and the preferences of peers and direct reports. These managers are listed among the people who are least often joked with and also least often joked about by others. In the rare instances when they are included in the joking pattern, they are customarily the butt of the joke. As these managers are arrogant, jokes about them are obviously told when they are absent.

Arrogant executives are not considered friends. In fact, they are the least liked members of the group. When group members are asked to imagine themselves in a position of leadership and to select their own followers, the arrogant manager is never chosen. A joke told about an employee is more offensive to others if it is told by the arrogant executive than if it is initiated by any other member of the group.

The Benign Bureaucrat

This manager is not isolated from colleagues or from other employees. Employees at all levels freely tell jokes to benign bureaucrats and even make them the butt of jokes in their presence. It may be that benign bureaucrats are included while joking because group members perceive them as powerless to do anything about the jokes despite their formal authority.

Group members do not respect a manager who has authority but who fails to exercise it. Benign bureaucrats are rejected when group members are asked to choose those they prefer as leaders, and their performance is consistently perceived as the worst in the group. Like the arrogant executive, the benign bureaucrat offends others if he or she tells jokes about employees. However, the reason for offense is different in this case: the benign bureaucrat's joke is resented because he or she is not respected as a productive member of the group. But in the case of the arrogant executive, the person cracking the joke is simply not liked.

The Solid Citizen

The solid citizen is the group's 'Good Old Boy or Girl'. He or she does not possess formal authority and is socially close to other members of the work group. In direct opposition to the benign bureaucrat, who has authority without power, the solid citizen has power but no authority over the other group members. His or her power stems from perceived expertise; fellow workers select the solid citizen more often than they select anyone else as the 'best' employee in the group.

The solid citizen is also chosen as the preferred leader

and when group members are asked who they would like as followers, the solid citizen is the first choice. He or she enjoys special joking privileges; they can joke about group members, even in their presence, without offending anyone. In fact, group members like being close enough to this hero to be joked about by him or her. But solid citizens must also learn to be good sports, since their peers choose them as the people they are most likely to joke about. Clearly, a good sense of humour is an essential trait for this popular group member and, in fact, it is probably one of the reason for his or her popularity.

Novice

The novice is often the target for joking, that is, not the butt but the audience or receiver. The novice is younger than most of the other members of the group, is likely to be a newcomer to the organization, and has no managerial authority. As because the novice has no experience and no authority, he or she is perceived, along with the benign bureaucrat, to be a poor performer. The other group members recognize that the novice is powerless and non-threatening, and they freely include him or her in the pattern of joking relationships. To make a novice the butt of a joke, however, is considered tasteless, at least until he or she has had a chance to become known and accepted by the group. Even though novices are parties to many jokes, they rarely joke with or about others, and they almost never dare make an established group member the butt of a joke.

When it comes to the frequency of humour with different type of colleagues, age and work experience are very relevant. It can be noticed that the more young employees are, the more they prefer having humour-based relationships with their peers, while seasoned people have almost no preferences—all colleagues are equal when it comes to humour. The reason for that could be that young people may think that trying to joke with their superiors may be counterproductive for their career. It is very interesting to notice a kind of peculiar behaviour shown by people in their forties. They are the only group that show a higher percentage of humour with their superiors compared to subordinates. Given the fact that for many people their forties is when important achievements in career happen, it might be that people of this age group prefer to limit their humour to subordinates in order to protect their still 'unstable' leadership position, on the other hand they engage in humour-based relationships with their superior in order to show that they are 'part of that lucky group'.

Types of Humour at the Workplace

Types of workplace humour is definitely multifaceted; in fact, it can take the form of jokes, irony, sarcasm, stories, wordplays, puns, anecdotes etc. Below is an (partial) inventory of the different flavours that humour may have, with some comments. However, different categories may overlap.

Types of Humour	Comments and Examples
Spontaneous and conversational humour	This is by far the most dominant type of humour at the workplace. Humour usually comes out unplanned, based on what is going on in a specific moment.
Unintentional humour	Unintentional humour is very funny but sometimes is also based on a good deal of aggressiveness, since it very often means laughing at other people's mistakes or strange behaviour.
Jokes	Jokes are not very common in workplace. However, if you are not very good at spontaneous conversational humour, knowing many jokes can help you in being humorous. However, you should

	also be able to tell jokes since its effectiveness is not only based on the content but also on body language, narration style and voice.
Stories and anecdotes	Stories and anecdotes, if used properly, are very effective. However, one issue with it is if they are based on your personal experience, sometimes it may seem that you want to show off. Usually,
	they are more frequent than jokes and less than spontaneous conversational humour.
Wordplay	Wordplay humour is quite frequent. Depending on how you play with words it can be very effective, but also very ineffective. Sometimes people consider wordplay humour a polite way to be humorous, but it can be impolite and aggressive too. For example: 'Did you receive the customer contract?' 'Yes, but it was too contracted.' (meaning too short)
Pun	Pun is a specific type of wordplay. It means using a word that brings up a humorous second meaning. This humour is usually based on a homophone, a word that sounds the same but has a different meaning. For example: 'Did you read the document I sent you yesterday? What did you think of it?' 'Yes, I did. It had a lot of comma sense!'
Funny sayings	Funny sayings can be effective if you do not use them too often, otherwise the result maybe a little bit boring and it may seem that you want to show off you knowledge. For example: Edgar Bergen once said, 'Hard work never killed anybody, but why take a chance?'

Transformation of frozen expressions	It means changing well-known sayings and clichés into unique sayings. It is not a very common source of humour, but when it happens, it is usually quite funny. In addition, it is also easy to remember and retrieve since it is based on famous quotes/sayings. For example: 'He who laughs last, didn't get it.'
Double entendre	A double entendre is a figure of speech in which a spoken phrase is intended to be understood in either of 2 ways. In most cases, the first meaning is straightforward, while the second meaning is often sexual or inappropriate. For example, the famous dialogue from *The Silence of the Lambs*: Hannibal Lecter: 'I do wish we could chat longer, but… I'm having an old friend for dinner. Bye.' In case you do not know, Hannibal is actually having—as in eating—a friend for dinner, instead of just having a friend over to eat dinner together.
Freudian slip	In humour, a Freudian slip is typically an 'unintentional' error in speech or reading. According to the classical psychoanalysis, it is interpreted as an occurrence due to the interference of an unconscious (dynamically repressed) subdued wish, conflict, or train of thought guided by the ego and the rules of correct behaviour. It reveals a 'source outside the speech'. For example: An employee was working the night shift. At the end of the shift he went to his supervisor and said: 'I have finished my work shit, may I go home?'
Irony	Irony is when there is an incongruity or discordance between what one says or does and what one means or what is generally understood.

Types of Humour at the Workplace ■ 67

For example:
After the presentation of a colleague, someone asked: 'Clear enough?'
Another colleague: 'Yes, clear as the night.'

Sarcasm — Sarcasm is a cutting, often ironic remark intended to express contempt or ridicule.
For example:
A person sits at her desk and she notices that one of her co-workers is talking loudly on his phone. When the co-worker hangs up, she remarks, 'I think you should talk a little bit louder next time, the entire office didn't quite hear it.'

Teasing — Teasing is a humorous remark directed at the listener. Unlike sarcasm, the intention is not to seriously offend or insult anyone.
For example:

An employee knows and jokes about his own very bad handwriting. One of his colleagues asked him to take notes during a meeting. On submitting the notes, his colleague replied to him: 'Thank you very much! I guess it has been very difficult to take notes with your feet!'

Inventing funny scenarios — It means creating unrealistic or very improbable funny scenarios. Unlike jokes, it is not very common.
For example:
One of your colleagues is a very strong technician but with very low communication skills. In addition, he dresses very shabbily. Speaking

about him, another colleague comments: 'Can you imagine him working in the sales department? I guess he has to pay the customers to retain them!'

Generating implicatures	Generating implicatures means conveying, implying, or suggesting a meaning without directly expressing it.

For example:
Let us consider Gaurav, a colleague with a very rich family, who is used to very expensive restaurants. He had been invited by his supervisor for lunch in order to discuss a project. The restaurant that the supervisor had selected was one of the worst in the neighbourhood, but Gaurav was not aware of that. A colleague, seeing them leave the company at lunch time, exclaimed: 'Gaurav, maybe I am mistaken, but you are on a diet from today, right?' Gaurav, not aware of what was going on, replied: 'Actually, no. I am very hungry!' All the colleagues, aware of how Gaurav was not going to enjoy the lunch, silently laughed. |
| Exaggerating | Exaggerating means to consider, represent, or cause to appear as larger, more important, or more extreme a situation or fact than is actually the case.
For example:
Consider a company that runs many stores. Stores are connected to the headquarter by VPN (Virtual Private Network). If the connection does not work, stores cannot see whether a product that a customer wants but is not available in that store, is available in other stores or not. Normally, this scenario is the exception and not the rule. One day the VPN was down for two hours. A salesperson asked: 'Do we have any data about the impact of the non-availability of VPN on sales and customers?' A colleague replied: 'Customers? We no longer have customers; all of them changed suppliers during those 2 hours!' |

Types of Humour at the Workplace ▪ 69

Performing
: Performing means imitating, and normally exaggerating the mannerisms of another person.

  This is quite an aggressive type of humour since it makes fun of the behaviour that is considered different from the norm. Performing usually happens when the target person is not present. For example:

  Suman, an employee, pronounces the letter S in a way very similar to the letter F. A colleague (to mock Suman) called another colleague by phone and said: 'Hallo, forry if I difturb you. I waf looking for Fuman, have you feen him fomewhere?'

Pranks
: A prank is a mischievous trick or joke, especially one in which something is done rather than said. Sometimes pranks aim to put down the target persons, in other cases it is just a way to strengthen bonds among colleagues. In some companies, to pranksomeone is a way to say: 'Now you are part of our group, we accept you.'

  Here is one of the best pranks I have seen in a corporate environment:

  A newly hired salesperson received a formal invitation letter stating this: 'Dear Sir, we are happy to inform you that you have been selected from among our employees to attend the Magic Night Gala Dinner. The dinner is meant to be a networking event, in fact, all of our main customers have been invited. Please note, formal dress (tuxedo) is mandatory.' Of course, the Gala Dinner did not exist and all the salespeople were aware of the prank, so when the colleague disclosed the invitation the typical replies were: 'You are very lucky, I have worked in this company for 10 years but I never received the invitation to the Gala Dinner.

Honestly I am a little bit envious, however, good for you!' The Gala Dinner was supposed to be almost 100 km far from the company, in an amazing hotel. The salesperson, with his very classy (and rented) tuxedo went there and, inevitably, the receptionists of the hotel could only communicate that no Gala Dinners were planned. The day after, all the salesperson's colleagues asked him how the party was. He tried to act as if the prank did not bother him but it was clear that the opposite was true. In the end, it emerged that all the new salespeople went through the same prank; it was a kind of 'welcome among us' ritual.

Picture — In many offices, through cubicles and email communications, pictures are a source of humour. As I will mention later in the chapter related to the negative side of humour, pictures that represent dissatisfaction against some aspect of the job can be counterproductive both for the person that uses it and also the company as a whole.

Gesture — Humour can also be based on gestures. Imitating the gestures of other people, distorted facial expressions, and body reactions to fearful events or threats, exaggerating a fact by means of your body. For example: If you repetitively ask a fisherman to show you how big the fish he caught was, you will see the dimension of the fish growing by way of his hands.

Satire — Satire is a form of aggressive humour that pokes fun at social institutions and public policy. A satire can also be aimed at an organization and its source of power (top managers). However, this type of humour is residual.

For example:

The chairman of a company was known for his rude manners and for showing off his power. The company had a large courtyard and employees started to use it as a parking lot. Cars in the courtyard had a negative impact on the aesthetic look of the company's building but employees were very happy to have the opportunity to park so close to their office. One day, an official communication arrived by email to all the employees: 'With effect from today, it is strictly forbidden to park in the courtyard.' The email was signed by the chairman. For the next few days nobody parked in the courtyard except for two or three cars that were still there, so the other employees too began to park in the courtyard again some days after having received the communication. Then a new communication arrived by email, reinforcing the message that parking in the courtyard was forbidden. In addition, notices stating 'No parking' had been displayed in the courtyard. However, two to three cars still remained there. They were the chairman's cars. One day someone added to the 'No parking' notices in the courtyard: 'This does not apply to the Chairman. This is a lead-by-example company!'

Replies to rhetorical questions

Rhetorical questions are not meant to be answered. Answering a rhetorical question creates incongruity and a reversal of expectations.

For example:

In order to indicate that a colleague is very fast in carrying out his/her tasks, Alok said: 'She is faster than the speed of light!' Anticipating no response and a clear expectation that the person understands what has been communicated, another colleague replied, 'It is impossible. The relativity theory states that speed of light cannot be reached and even less exceeded!'

Normally, this type of humour is not very funny (annoying?) and it is very rare.

Clever replies to serious statements	These are clever and nonsensical replies to a question that was meant to be serious. For example: During a job interview, the candidate may ask: 'How is the salary here?' The interviewer replies: 'Enough to survive, sometimes enough to resign!'
Making fun of yourself	As already mentioned, self-defeating humour is quite common in many organizations and it can be a way to shorten the power distance. However, sometimes it is used with an opposite purpose: I can make fun of myself but you cannot. I decide what is funny about me, not you. For example: Meeting scheduled at 9 a.m. The boss was late, he arrived at 9.20. He was quite overweight. He entered the meeting room and said: 'Sorry for being late, but if I do not have a sumptuous breakfast I cannot start the day!'
Making fun of other people	Making fun of other people is very common in every company. In theory, it can be considered an aggressive style of humour, but in practice it really depends on how you implement it. However, in the long run, it can be annoying if the butt of jokes is always the same person. For example: At the vending machine of a consultancy company, an employee always used small-denomination

coins. One day, he was approaching the vending machine with a pile of coins when one of his colleagues said: 'Is your wife aware that you steal from poor people? This time I will pay for you, but please give the money back to the owner!'

Making fun of work roles	Making fun of work roles is also quite common in many organizations. Work roles can be related to specific people (the CEO of the company) but very often they represent generalizations—marketing people, IT people, etc. On the internet you can find tons of jokes related to work roles.

For example:

One employee asked another one: 'It is more than 2 months since I saw Aditi's husband. Do you have any news?'

He replied: 'I guess she sold him to reach the sales target! This is quite common among salespeople!'

Violating social rules/ conventions/ norms	All the organizations have some rules, conventions, norms. They are similar to sources of power and authority because they impose specific behaviour. And since the recorded history, source of power and authority are good inputs for humour.

For example:

In a company there was a photocopier that all the employees could use. The written rule (emailed and stuck on the wall) was: 'Please, always refill the photocopier with the same amount of paper that you use.' One day the photocopier did not work. The person trying to use it opened the tray to check if there was paper and found a paper notebook inside with the following note: 'I used 10 sheets only, you can keep the rest!'

Playing with gender differences	In some companies and countries, this type of humour is avoided; in others it is tolerated. For sure, it is a risky territory and it has to be handled with care. For example: It is quite a common stereotype that women, when they have to travel, carry bigger baggage compared to men. A female employee had to travel for business for just 2 days. In order to go to the airport, she asked for a taxi. One of her male colleagues said: 'Remember to specify that you need a mini-van, cars cannot handle your baggage! Did you pack the kitchen as well?'
Sexual humour	If the above mentioned type of humour should be handled with care, then sexual humour should be avoided altogether. Risks very often exceed benefits. For example: A software programmer, trying to joke about the ample bosom of his colleague, told her: 'Please sit a little bit farther from the keyboard, you are inserting too many spaces in the code with your breasts!'
Bad words humour	For many people bad words are just part of their communication style and in many organizations they are not so uncommon. Bad words typically are funny when they cause incongruence with the situation/person. For example: A colleague of mine is a very calm person. In addition, her name is Angel, perfectly aligned with her character. One day, after a call with a very

annoying person, she ended the call by repeating: 'Thank you…thank you…thank you.' Once the call was over she said: 'you should say thank you that I did not shoot you in your ass face!' It was hilarious because seeing her so rude was very incongruous with her personality.

Playing with cultural differences	This type of humour is present when there are different behaviours and languages among different countries, different parts of the country, and even among different companies. When this type of humour is based on stereotypes, it can be used as a mechanism to strengthen relationships among colleagues or to benignly underline deviant behaviours. However, you should be careful when using this type of humour since it can also be offensive, especially if repeated too often. For example: Many consultants use the term 'deliverable' too often and without a real clue of what a deliverable actually is. In consultancy, normally deliverables are associated to payments from the client organization. Once a consultant went to the toilet and an employee of the client organization said: 'Are you going to charge this deliverable as well?'
Playing with religions	Please, never do that. Full stop.

The Positive Side of Humour at the Workplace

Stress Management and Stress Perception

First of all, what is stress? Stress is an adaptive response, moderated by individual differences, that is a consequence of any action, situation, or event, which places special demands on a person.

Almost everyone knows that people and teams under stress underperform. Stress has been shown to create unhealthy physiological changes. On the physiological side, the connection between stress and high blood pressure, muscle tension and immunosuppression are well documented. Even on the psychological side, stress outcomes such as emotional disturbance, cognitive inefficiency and behavioural impairment are well known.

In any case, these negative outcomes are not unavoidable; there are mental mechanisms that help in better managing life's stressful events.

Humour has been considered since long a tool for

helping managing stressful events. Norman Dixon, a British psychologist and author, even asserted that human beings have developed humour just for this purpose.

Have you ever noticed that doctors and nurses use humour to target at patients and/or serious diseases, and normally that kind of humour is considered inappropriate? Well, they use humour not because they want to make fun of patients, but because humour permits them to confront themselves with situations that otherwise will cause an unmanageable source of stress.

Functional Magnetic Resonance Imaging (FMRI) scans show that laughter changes the biochemistry of our brain and hormonal system. The use of humour, in stressful situations, decreases our heart rate, blood pressure and muscle tension. It helps us to increase infection-fighting antibodies and has a positive effect on our immune system.

Humour helps in reducing stress because it allows people to change one's point of view about a problem, enabling them to see it from a different prospective, since it usually involves incongruities and multiple interpretations. It, thus, offers the opportunity to explore cognitive alternatives in response to stressful situations and to reduce the negatively affecting consequences. This property, not only permits to reduce stress in a given situation, but also allows people to deal with stressful situations that otherwise could be very difficult to tolerate.

Stress: The PC

Aditi has to send an email to her boss by 9.10 in the morning. 9.10 is mandatory since at that time the boss will have a conference call with a customer and she realizes that she does not have the latest version of a contract.

9.04—the email does not open: it is asking for the password.

9.04–9.06—after having inserted the password 12 times, Aditi realizes that the current password expired during the previous night.

9.07—Aditi follows the online procedure to change the password.

9.08—now Aditi is able to access the email. She is very nervous. Time is almost over. She opens the email and attaches the contract. An alert warns Aditi that the file cannot be attached. Aditi yells at the PC: 'Come on! What's the problem? What's wrong with you?'

9.09—Aditi tries to reattach the file. After a few seconds the same alert pops up: 'Unable to attach the file'. Aditi says to the PC: 'Listen, if you do not take the file I am going to transform you from International Business Machines to Idiot Burning Machines!' She laughs alone and suddenly she realizes that the company has capped the email attachment to 10 MB.

9:10—Aditi zips the file and finally she is able to send it to her boss.

In this case, at the peak level of stress, using humour permitted to Aditi to lower the tension and to shift the focus of her brain, thus, broadening her perspective. In this way, she was able to exit from the vicious circle 'you have to take this attachment' from 'why does it not work?' She knew the rule of the maximum dimension of the attachments but she was so focused and stressed, that she was not able to recall the rule from her memory. Humour was the answer.

Along with problem solving, studying the effects of humour should include the distinction between the effects of humour as a personality trait variable (the so-called sense of humour) and the effects of humour as a reaction to humorous stimuli.

From the first perspective humorous people are skilled in rapid perceptual-cognitive switches in frames or references, an ability that presumably enables them to reappraise a problematic situation, distance themselves from its immediate threat, and thereby reduce the often paralyzing feelings of anxiety and helplessness. This is relevant when recruiting new people—humorous people are not only useful to improve the organizational climate, but usually they are also good problem solvers, thus, increasing the ability of the organization to navigate through rough seas.

From the second perspective, it is clear that stimulating colleagues with humour has beneficial factors when it comes to stress management. A study by Millicent Abel and David Maxwell has shown that individuals who watch a humorous video inducing mirth, experienced greater reduction in state anxiety and improvement in positive affect than those viewing a non-humorous video.

In another study, Michelle Newman and Arthur Stone asked a group of students to write either a serious story or a humorous one while they were watching a video of bloody accidents. The students writing humorous stories showed a lower level of emotional distress as well as lower skin conductivity, a slower pulse and a higher temperature compared to the other group—all of these signals to reduced stress.

From a mere financial perspective, there is also the fact that stress is a common cause of illness and leads to underperforming; so stimulating the use of humour can help improve productivity.

Creativity and Problem Solving

Humour is often considered as an expression of creativity, since its 'ingredients' such as incongruity, novelty and surprise are very similar to the ones of a work of art or any other intellectual work, which are typically associated with the concept of creativity.

Humour is able to moderately increase creativity. Humour encourages creative thinking by making people less prone to criticize new ideas or to point out others' mistakes and less exposed to stress. People under stress tend to replicate their behavioural patterns and to ignore alternative approaches in the accomplishment of a task, especially if it is particularly complex.

This positive approach supports risk-taking behaviour, which is one of the pillars of creative thinking. A humour-filled atmosphere instils a contagious positive mood thanks to which novel ideas are more likely to come out.

Avner Ziv, a researcher and author, made some students listen to comic pieces, while another group was involved in non-comic activities. The 2 groups were then asked to take a test on verbal creativity. Students exposed to the comic pieces achieved better results in fluency, flexibility, originality and generally speaking, in creativity.

In another study, students were split into groups. One of the groups watched a humorous film, another watched a neutral film and a third one watched no film at all. They were then asked to complete a task that involved using problem-solving skills. The number of subjects who watched the humorous film and successfully completed the task was 55 per cent more than the neutral film group and 62 per cent more than the group that watched no film at all.

Other researchers have studied the relationship between positive emotions and creativity. Even though positive emotions are a broader set comparing to humour, the method often adopted to elicit them was by watching a comic film. Even under these circumstances, the results confirmed that humour increases creativity and problem-solving. Interestingly, though, the same result has been achieved also using non-humoristic methods to elicit positive emotions.

As a result, it seems that the increase in creativity is caused by the emotional state driven by humour and not by a specific aspect of humour, that is, the activation of multiple mind frames, typical of the generation and appreciation of humour. The decline in strain and anxiety due to humour can make one's mind less strict, and thus, more ready to integrate different ideas.

The creativity of a single individual supports the creativity of the team, thus, when creative tasks have to be performed, humour can play a role. Humour seems to also enhance creative problem-solving, a finding supported by some organizations such as Google, Yahoo, Pixar Animation Studios, which have created a playful workplace environment to support creativity. Self-enhancing and affiliative humour are the most suitable types of humour to foster creativity. The use of affiliative humour supports creativity by creating an open environment where ideas can be freely expressed without negative criticism, while self-enhancing humour encourages creative thinking by reducing the importance of failed attempts.

Increasing the customer satisfaction and revenues through creativity

Queuing at supermarkets and stores, is an issue especially in big cities where people have long working days. They are stressed, and as a result they do not want to waste their time while waiting in a queue. Too long queues cause the customers to abandon their purchases and decrease the probability that the customer will show up again at the same store. Refer to the following example:

A meeting to discuss how to reduce the abandon rate while standing in queue at the supermarket. People attending the meeting: Area Manager, acting as the coordinator of the meeting and 6 Store Managers, acting as people that should provide ideas in order to find a solution.

Area Manager: 'We recently noticed that in our urban stores the number of people that abandon the queue while waiting to pay has increased. In rural areas this is not an issue, but in urban areas we have estimated that we are losing 4–6 per cent of the turnover due to customers that abandon queues. We have to find a solution!'

Store Manager 1: 'Why not simply add some more counters?'

Area Manager: 'In your store that is possible since we can afford additional costs and there is enough room to add 1 or 2 counters more, but in the other stores we do not have that space and money to do so.'

Store Manager 2: 'One of the issues I noticed is that people remove the items from their baskets directly at the counters and this slows down the process. We should install counters with long conveyor belts in order to let customers lay their items before the check-out.'

Area Manager: 'I agree with you, but I see your proposal applicable only in the long term. We cannot change the counters right now, they are too expensive. In some stores, we do not even have enough room to accommodate those types of counters.'

Store Manager 3 (smiling): 'We should provide a karaoke, customers can sing while waiting!'

All the other laughed and a humorous chain started.

Store Manager 4: 'Or you could train the cashiers to sing!'

Store Manager 5: 'Or you can even hire a cheap singer! Abhira, of the cleaning company, will be happy to sing for us! (Abhira loves to sing while working but her performance is not the best...)

Store Manager 6: 'Oh gosh, Abhira no! Do you want to lose all the customers?'

Store Manager 1: 'However, entertaining the customers can be a solution! As we have understood, working on reducing queues can be unfeasible in the short run, maybe we can just find a way to make the customer believe that the queues are not that long by making them less boring. As you know, time flies when you are having fun!'

Area Manager: 'And so, any ideas?'

Store Manager 3: 'Free newspapers?'

Store Manager 4: 'What about a television showing candid cameras?'

Area Manager: 'That makes sense. I am thinking about the situation in the other stores and I do not see any problems. Also, the cost is very low. Okay, let's go for it!'

As you can see, humour did not create directly the solution to the problem but it improved the ability to think

> out of the box and to see the problem from a different perspective. Store Manager 3 was not aware he was contributing to the solution but Store Manager 1 linked the gag to the idea of entertaining the customers. Store Manager 4 then found the solution.

Motivation

The way humour supports motivation is not direct but indirect. For example, humour can contribute in increasing motivation by alleviating the boredom of work and by helping employees to find a meaning in their job while making a game out of it. Another indirect effect of humour on motivation is through the role it plays on hope. Hope can be defined as any probability to attain a goal that is greater than zero, and it is made up by 2 elements—agency and pathways. Agency can be defined as the feeling of performing a goal, which is both important and reachable. Pathways refers to the ability of finding the most effective way to reach the goal, according to the specific characteristics of the context. Positive emotions lead to a momentary broadening of the thought-action spectrum. Humour being a positive emotion, it can lead to an expansion of the thought-action repertoire, leading to a greater sense of self-efficacy for dealing with specific problems or stressful events. In this way, humour positively enhances both agency and pathways, thus, increasing the sense of hope and, in turn, motivation.

More generally, it can be reasonably expected that by enhancing communication, reducing conflicts, facilitating negotiations, etc., humour can positively impact motivation through the creation of a more positive working environment. It must be taken into account, however, that an unscrupulous use of humour by leaders could make subordinates perceive set goals as not serious and, thereby, reduce their motivation instead of increasing it.

> **Motivation: When humour does not help**
>
> The marketing department of a company that builds and sells appliances had decided to campaign an offer of supplying refrigerators with additional colours, at a premium price. The idea was to increase sales and especially profitability, which unfortunately were declining year by year. Traditionally refrigerators are white, sometimes grey, but rarely ever in other colours. The marketing department decided to introduce these colours: yellow, red, blue and green. The next steps were to select the suppliers of the paints and to modify some production processes.
>
> The head of the production department called for a meeting to present the project to his team and to discuss the next few steps.
>
> He opened the meeting with this statement: 'The marketing department decided to provide our refrigerators in additional colours: yellow, red, blue and green. I was not aware that our main customer was Barbie!'
>
> In this case, the head of the production department made a mistake by using humour. The situation was serious; the company was losing profitability and had to find a way to improve it. Even if the he did not believe in the project, he did not have to make fun of it. In this way, the message conveyed was something like: 'This project is rubbish but we have to do it. Please do not waste too much time, we have other priorities.'

It also seems that people with a high sense of humour also have a bigger motivation in performing tasks. In one study, participants were asked to complete 2 drawing tasks and to provide their cognitive evaluation both before and after their performance. Results showed that individuals with a higher sense of humour showed more positive challenge appraisals for both the tasks, and lower negative appraisals before the first draw. Furthermore, it was found that individuals with a greater sense of humour had a higher level of motivation and showed more positive feelings towards the task.

Communication and Message Recall

Humour enhances communication by creating a more open environment and evoking positive emotions that, in turn, improve listening, reciprocal understanding and message reception. In educational settings, for example, humour is often encouraged to be used as a pedagogical tool, though mainly as a way to increase students' positive associations with the class. Humour enhances communication not only by creating a positive atmosphere, but also by facilitating the transfer of messages otherwise difficult or risky to pass.

Communication and message recall: Selling project management

Apart from humour, my specialization is project management. When I speak with managers and top managers, they are well aware of the importance of this topic for the performance of their companies. I teach undergraduate students to simply trust me, so that they do not have to stress on the importance of project management

> in the business world. Sometimes problems arise when it comes to graduate students, especially if enrolled in 'career boosting' programmes such as MBA. Since MBA students dream of being top managers, they have a natural tendency to prefer courses that make them dream—strategy, marketing and finance are some examples. Project management, together with other practical disciplines, is less 'sexy'. Hence, one of the first steps in order to be successful in teaching project management is convincing participants that the topic matters.
>
> I have a lot of quantitative data that shows that project management is a key ingredient in every company, but still that data is not very able at catching the attention of the participants and engaging them.
>
> Then I found a better way: humour. When the course begins, I show a slide with this motto: 'Vision without execution is hallucination!' This sentence is from the book *The Mind of the CEO* and it is attributed to Stephen Case, former Chairman and CEO of America Online. Since it is a quite humorous sentence, it grabs the attention of the participant and it conveys 2 important messages—project management is strategy's close friend and important CEOs believe so.
>
> The final results are: increase the attractiveness of the topic and also the ability to remember the message for a long time.

Humour, indeed, thanks to its ambiguous nature, welcomes critiques and potentially offensive comments without causing negative interrelation effects. The intrinsic ambiguity of humour helps to overcome the opposition that people usually show when they feel criticized, because the critique becomes the source of a shared laugh. In fact, when people share humour they are less likely to get offended by each other and are, thus, more open to an honest conversation.

> ### Communication: Good work! Or not...
>
> Mrs Pansari was in charge of collecting and analysing marketing data in Excel. As discussed with her supervisor, she sent the Excel file by email on Wednesday night.
>
> The day after she met her supervisor and asked: 'Did you see any errors in the worksheet I sent you?'
>
> The supervisor replied, smiling: 'Yes, only 3. Your data, formulas and format!'
>
> Mrs Pansari laughed.
>
> The supervisor added: 'Actually there are some issues, let's see them together.'
>
> Mrs Pansari took a seat and listened to the suggestions of her supervisor.
>
> Actually, the supervisor was not satisfied with the job that Mrs Pansari did. In order to communicate the negative outcome in a less threatening way, she decided to use humour based on exaggeration. In this way Mrs Pansari reacted with a laugh, since her supervisor was smiling and it was impossible to believe that everything was wrong. The supervisor, too, was able to explain the real issues without eliciting a defence mind-set in Mrs Pansari. In fact, if her supervisor had replied with: 'Your worksheet is a disaster, there are many issues!' probably Mrs Pansari would have felt 'under attack' and the typical reaction on such occasions is trying to defend what you did, without really listening to what the supervisor was saying.

Furthermore, almost paradoxically, humorous stories about misunderstandings promote effective communication. Therefore, humour can enhance the transfer of information, alleviate message-related frustration and introduce new data.

Several studies on humour conducted in the advertising field suggest that humour also has an attention-grabbing quality that enhances comprehension, persuasion and emotional associations. Use of humour in advertisements boosts initial attention, helps brand recall and keeps interest high among viewers.

The impact of humour on the communication of a message depends also on the humour quotient (i.e. 'how funny' it is) and, in particular, on how much it relates to the message. For instance, a radio commercial where humour is associated with the product is perceived as more interesting by the audience than one in which it isn't. Similarly, advertisements (ads) in which humour is related to the product are easier to recall over ads in which humour is independently used.

In particular, ads are easier to remember when humour quotient is high, but this recall is also mediated by audience's attention and mood. Self-enhancing humour, in particular, is often used in commercials to form a connection with the audience, but moderate self-defeating humour is also sometimes employed to make the audience feel closer to the product sponsored by reducing the status of the advertiser. Affiliative humour can also be used to create more empathy between the speaker and the audience by focusing on similarities.

However, humour does not always have a positive effect on memory. Contrasting results come from studies in educational settings, which show that humour increased students' participation and interest in the class but did not improve their memory. These conflicting findings regarding the relationship between humour and memory may be explained by the fact that humour does not have a direct effect on memory, but it works indirectly through other mechanisms, such as rehearsal, surprise and incongruity. Therefore, leaders who need to effectively communicate important messages (for e.g. a change in the vision or in the company culture) to their subordinates can reach their intent by employing humour, however, it must be related to the message, appropriate to the characteristics of the target, and able to generate interest.

Test of Acceptable Boundaries

Humour can be used as a means to test other people's preferences as well as a way to understand which are the limits that cannot be crossed without obtaining a negative response from the others. This approach is usually applied during the phase of group formation, that is, the period of time when people who are working in a group do not know each other thoroughly. Many topics, if faced up to, may generate tension or obtain just convenient answers, which lacks in truthfulness. Sexual orientation, political and religious tendencies are topics that, generally, should be treated very carefully, otherwise they may lead to slowing down of the formation process of a work group.

The use of a playful tone during a conversation allows the speaker to dissociate him/herself from what has been said, thus, 'saving his/her face'; humour actually allows oneself to enter into debating arguments that are otherwise difficult. Humour provides what I call the 'parachute', that is a higher level of safety regarding a concept which will not be accepted well by the listener if discussed seriously.

> **Test of acceptable boundaries: The zoo**
>
> An employee in the HR department of an organization who provided training services had been appointed as the new head of HR. Among his first tasks, he recruited a new young employee. One morning, while walking along the corridor to reach his office, a senior employee saw the newly hired person and he started to talk to him. It took him a few minutes to realize that the new person was not very smart. He then continued walking along the corridor.
>
> When he saw the boss, he said: 'Dear boss, I saw that we are expanding the zoo!'—meaning that he was comparing the intelligence of the new person to that of an animal's and also that the whole organizational unit was not in a good shape.
>
> The facial expression of the boss changed suddenly, indicating he did not appreciate the joke.
>
> Promptly, the senior employee who made the statement added: 'Of course, I am the oldest monkey here!'
>
> In this way, he rolled back the comment by comparing himself to another animal.
>
> The boss's face then returned to a more relaxed expression.

Ingratiation

Ingratiation can be defined as an attempt to increase one's attractiveness and power of influence upon others. Being a typical aspect of social interactions, ingratiation is particularly pervasive in any organization. People may adopt ingratiatory behaviour towards their superiors, co-employees or subordinates to achieve various objectives, such as to be helped, to get rewards, or simply to be liked. The interpersonal attraction theory maintains that people are attracted to each other according to the extent to which they generate positive feelings or are associated with another stimulus that generates positive emotions. Based on what I have already mentioned, humour has the power to generate positive feelings in the target, therefore, humour exerts an ingratiatory function through this mechanism. Humour, indeed, can be used to gain people's attention, seek favours and, more generally, to be liked by others. In particular, self-enhancing humour is functional when addressing higher status members of an organization, while self-disparaging humour can be useful to grab lower-status employees' attention and getting closer to them.

The effectiveness of any ingratiatory behaviour depends, on the target's perception of the ingratiatior's intent. The least risky ingratiation technique based on humour is simply laughing at the gags proposed by the target.

If the ingratiatory attempt is overt to the target, it is much less likely to be successful and more likely to cause a decrease—rather than an increase—of interpersonal liking. However, being a less evident ingratiatory tactic compared to others, humorous expressions are less likely to seem hypocrite or manipulative.

Ingratiation: Not always effective

On a very hot and humid afternoon in Chennai:

In order to try to sell additional services, ABC, an Indian organization providing IT services, invited 2 customer representatives of one of their biggest clients.

The customer representatives enter the company and

3 persons from ABC welcomed them. Among the persons from ABC, 2 were seniors, the third one was a junior and it was his first time participating in a sales meeting. The senior colleagues already warned him no to actively participate, but to just listen and be kind.

Customer representatives arrived. They were sweating a lot.

The senior-most person from ABC said: 'Good afternoon Mr Gupta and Mr Shankar. How are you?'

Mr Shankar, the person sweating the most, replied with a gentle smile: 'I would have preferred having a meeting in Srinagar!'

Among the 3 employees of ABC, the seniors replied with a gentle smile and the junior laughed.

They then approached the meeting room. One of the senior employees of ABC asked the customer representatives if they would like something to drink.

Mr Shankar: 'A very very hot cup of tea, please!'

Seniors from ABC replied with a broad smile and the junior again laughed loudly.

Mr Shankar said: 'Joking, if you have cold water it will be very fine, thank you.'

Once again, the junior employee of ABC laughed.

The meeting continued in this way—mild jests that asked for no more than a smile brought broad smiles and made the junior employee laugh.

The meeting ended with a plan to see each other again to delve deeper on some topics. After a few days, one of the senior employees called Mr Shankar to schedule the next meeting.

Mr Shankar replied: 'Okay, Monday afternoon, will the laughing guy be with us?' The message was loud and clear.

He replied: 'No, he is already scheduled on other tasks.'

In this case, it is clear that the attempt of the junior employee of ABC to be accepted by the customer representatives (and also by his senior colleagues) was a failure. It was clear that the reaction was not aligned with the intensity and quality of the gags.

The reaction of the senior employees were more appropriate and they were more effective ingratiation strategies. They used a passive strategy: just showing that they appreciated the jests of the guests without overacting.

Depending on the relationship between ABC senior employees and the client representatives, a more active technique could be replying to the gags with other gags.

Let's do an example.

ABC: 'Good afternoon Mr Gupta and Mr Shankar. How are you?'

Mr Shankar: 'I would have preferred having a meeting in Srinagar!'

ABC: 'Or to Ooty, it is closer!'

The problem with a more active ingratiation strategy is that you have to be ready to step back. In fact, many powerful people use humour to underline their status, so that they expect that you appreciate their humour but they do not like very much if you reply to their gags. In those cases, a suggestion is to see their reactions. If they reply with an authentic smile, probably the active strategy is working; if there is no smile or a fake smile, a more passive strategy is advisable.

When using humour as ingratiatory tactic it is also important to consider the context, especially in terms of both norms and culture. Group norms, i.e. those standards regulating group members' behaviour, may play a moderating role between humour and one's personal attraction towards the initiator. If humorous expressions are against the group norms, the effect of using humour as ingratiatory behaviour are obviously smaller, if not negative. Similarly, humour can be part of the culture of an organization and be expressed in its symbols, rituals, language or artefacts.

Since it is the culture that defines the values and behaviour of the members of an organization, it follows that the acceptance of joking behaviour at work depends on whether the organizational culture welcomes humour. Some companies have embraced humour as part of their culture, while other organizations stress the value of seriousness and formality and, in the latter, humorous ingratiatory behaviour must be adopted more carefully. In conclusion, managers and leaders can use humour as an ingratiatory tactic, either towards their subordinates or their superiors. But they must be aware of its potentialities, as well as those contextual factors that may affect negatively the effectiveness of their ingratiatory attempts.

Ingratiation: No need any longer

The boss was in a great mood. He narrated some jokes to the office staff. Everybody laughed uproariously, except for one woman.

'What's the matter with you?' asked the boss. 'Don't you have a sense of humour?'

'I don't have to laugh,' she replied. 'I am quitting on Friday!'

Group Identity, Climate and Cohesion

Every organization is made by people who contribute to its success not only as individuals, but also as part of functions, units and groups. Groups are often made by individuals who differ in terms of gender, age, culture and vision, but cohesiveness is one of the most important factors which determine the success of any team. In regard to this, humour has the ability to gather people together as it is a universal, social and cross-cultural phenomenon that is able to go beyond individual differences. Generally speaking, humour makes people feel part of the group, and joking behaviour is often implies a sense of belonging. Humour encourages group cohesiveness because it also represents a mutual interpretation of facts, and sharing a common vision makes the members of a group feel more closer to each other. Humour fosters group cohesiveness also by making the interactions of a socialization process less tense.

More specifically, group cohesiveness can be enhanced through the reinforcement of internal factors and the reduction of the external ones. On one hand, humour plays a role in supporting group cohesiveness by decreasing external threats and fostering members' ties. An example of such a situation is represented by members of a group who use aggressive humour to make jokes about their competitors. In accordance with the superiority theory, by ridiculing the external threat the group feels above and somehow triumphant over it.

Group identity: Damned salespeople!

Meeting of a production department:

The topic is how to deal with unplanned peaks of production caused by urgent customer orders. Participants: Head of the production department and 4 labourers involved in production planning and control.

Head of the production department said: 'Here we are again! Our dear sales department has signed another crazy contract. On top of the production we have already scheduled, we need additional 20,000 pieces of metal bars of 10×4 cms in 2 weeks. We have to find a solution for it!'

Labourer 1: 'I have it. We can teach salespeople to cut and finish metal bars. They can do the job during the night!'

Labourer 2: 'Teaching moulding and cutting to salespeople? Have you seen their hands? They look like they have just come from a beauty contest! The heaviest tool they have managed is a pen.'

(All the others laugh)

Labourer 3: 'A plastic pen! A metal pen would be too heavy for them!'

(Others laugh again)

Labourer 4: 'I guess they would cry for a month if they scratch a single fingernail of theirs!'

(Laughter)

Labourer 3: 'At the very least they will call an ambulance and will sue the company for having put their lives at risk!'

(More laughter)

In this case, it is clear usage of aggressive humour to put down the sales department and elevate the status, skills and behaviour of the production department. In addition, having a common target increases the sense of belonging.

On the other hand, humour may strengthen internal forces. Mild-aggressive humour, for example, may be used by senior members of an organization to initiate new members to the norms of the group so that the latter conforms and proves to be worthy of the group membership. Moreover, when some members of a group are ridiculed, the others are more likely to behave in accordance with the group norms. In such cases, managers should use affiliative and self-enhancing humour to foster norms. Affiliative humour, which is benevolent and focused on relationships, transforms the group in a trusted entity in which people are attracted to each other. Self-enhancing humour can improve the perception of the group that members have and create attachment to it. On the contrary, other types of humour that might cause denigration should be avoided, as the target person might feel excluded or discriminated rather than integrated in the group.

Group Identity: You are welcome!

The first meeting of a newly hired employee in the accounting department:

Colleagues in the accounting department have good relationships and they often joke about each other's appearances (dress, hairstyle, physical shape etc.). In the meeting room there are 10 senior colleagues and the new employee. Among the 10 colleagues, 7 are males and out of that 7, 3 are bald. The newly hired one is bald as well.

The meeting starts.

Senior male colleague 1, who is bald: 'Before starting the meeting, I would like to introduce you Mr Anand Sethia, our new colleague.'

Senior male colleague 2: 'But did you hire him because you want to outnumber people with hair on their head?'

(Laughter)

Senior male colleague 1: 'Even worse, it is part of a psychological strategy. The plan is to convince you to become bald as well.'

Senior male colleague 3: 'You will never have my hair! And, if I start losing my hair, I will just glue them back!'

(Laughter)

Senior female colleague 4: 'You always discuss about hair! It seems it is the most important thing in your life! Just relax!'

Senior male colleague 3: 'Easy for you, your head looks like the mane of a lion! You have so much hair that you can use your head as a penholder!

(Laughter)

Senior male 1: 'Okay, okay. Please Anand, just introduce yourself.'

Anand: 'Dear all, I am Anand. I am bald. Do not try to glue your hair, that's why I am bald!'

(Laughter)

In this case, it can be considered impolite to welcome a new colleague by using a type of humour related to the physical aspect, also because being bald can be the consequence of a disease, and in any case, it can be something that makes people feel uncomfortable. However, for Anand it was not a problem, and this funny and incautious welcome was very successful in making him feel part of the group since time zero. He was also very clever in linking his introduction to the previous gags; in this way, the rest of the group received the signal: 'Yes, you can joke with me, and I want to be a part of this group.'

A particular usage of humour is related to temporary groups (teams). A temporary group has a finite lifespan, formed around a shared and relatively clear goal or purpose, and its success depends on a tight and coordinated activity. With the growth of the 'contingency workforce' (where individuals work with a series of employers on specific assignments for limited time periods) and competitive pressures for greater adaptability and speed, temporary groups are becoming far more common in organizations. The challenge for a temporary group is to establish a sense of group cohesion and identity when the group faces a limited life span, the members tend to have limited experience of working with one another and limited prospects of doing so again, and the tasks tend to be non-routine. All this requires members to combine diverse capabilities and work interdependently toward a common goal. One of the challenges in a temporary group is to be effective in a short period of time: in other words, the socialization period should be shortened; trust should be created in a small timeframe.

Jenepheer Terrion and Blake Ashforth indicate that humour, and sometimes even put-down humour, plays a large role in melding individuals into a group. During a 6-week course for senior police officers they noticed that during it, humour changed, from self-disparaging to shared identities, then targeted to external groups and finally to in-group members, with different intensity based on the feedbacks of a single group member. Interestingly, even if the interpretation of the humorous situation was different from person to person, they believed that their interpretation would be shared by the other group members, thus creating a sense of cohesion.

Group members use humour to test, signal and reinforce

their growing trust and solidarity. Humour is a non-invasive way to test relations and give people a rollback mechanism (the parachute) in case of bad responses. On the other hand, a positive response boosts the use of humour in the other team members speeding up the socialization process. A joke can start a chain of humorous interpretations, giving the illusion of consensus to team members because they behave as if they share a common meaning. Further, humour, especially put-down humour, can be used in a ritualistic manner, where members subscribe to a set of implicit rules that preserved self and social esteem and facilitated a progressive sense of inclusion.

Humour can be also used to initiate conversations where there is little shared knowledge between the participants. In fact, a humorous comment can be the base for further conversation. In addition, it has been noted that a humorous comment made by one group member increases the group verbal participation immediately afterwards.

As proposed by Paul McGhee, 'Shared laughter and the spirit of fun generates a bonding process in which people feel closer together, especially when laughing in the midst of adversity. This emotional glue enables team members to stick together on the tough days, when members of the team need each other to complete a project and assure quality customer service.'

Humour strengthens group cohesion because when engaging in group interactions, group members use humour to control behaviour and form group norms. In addition, humour is a form of social pressure and encourages team members to conform to norms. Cohesion is also improved by the fact that humour represents a shared interpretation of events. This sharing highlights similarities among group members and creates a sense of equality among them. Moreover, humour creates bond among the employees thereby facilitating the accomplishment of work tasks.

However, humour can also have a negative effect on the socialization process. For example, frequent puns in response to ambiguous words can be disruptive and so can frequent joking, which distract participants from the topic and, due to the relatively long time that a joke takes, polarize the attention on a single group member. In these cases, a serious behaviour can be more appreciated than an aggressive or monopolistic use of humour.

Maintaining the Status and Hierarchy

Based on what we saw on humour and leadership and pattern of humour, it is not strange proposing that humour can be also used to strengthen one's status and emphasize his/her belonging to a specific hierarchical level. It has been noted that a person tends to laugh more in groups where one is in a dominant position compared to a situation in which the person has lesser power or a lower status, a typical ingratiation technique.

Rose Coser observed several meetings in a psychiatric hospital and she noticed that senior members generally used more humour that the junior ones did. She also observed that very often seniors' humoristic messages were directed towards the juniors and it included some sort of corrections or reprimands. On the other hand, junior staff members did not use humour towards senior members, rather they used self-deprecating humour, or making those people the target of their humour who were not present at the meeting. Dawn Robinson and Lynn Smith-Lovin noticed that people who tended to interrupt someone else frequently while he/she was speaking were also the people who create more humoristic situations. On the other hand, those who were often interrupted created less humoristic situations. Interestingly, during the first few phases of group formation, humour was used in order to define one's own status, and thus to establish hierarchy among the group.

> ### Maintaining the status and hierarchy: I am the leader, clear enough?
>
> A meeting between the head of sales department, Mrs Kapoor, and some of her subordinates:
>
> Sales declined by 2 per cent compared to the previous year, so the topic of the meeting was how to improve sales. The meeting started with a typical introduction and then the head of sales addressed the most important topic:
>
> 'Compared to the previous year we have lost 2 per cent of the sales while our target was to increase by 4 per cent, so we are 6 per cent far from the target. I would like to analyse with you the causes for this performance and the corrective actions to be implemented.'
>
> One of the subordinates replied: 'Sorry Mrs Kapoor, but our main competitors did worse than us, so we should be happy with the results we achieved!'
>
> Mrs Kapoor replied: 'Interesting point of view. Since other competitors have also reduced their workforce and we did not, I guess that if I reduce your salary by 30 per cent you should be more than happy! Right?'
>
> All the other people chuckled. For the rest of the meeting no one mentioned the performance of the competitors any longer.

> **Maintaining the status and hierarchy:**
> **I know I am a follower**
>
> Mr Rastogi, a white-collar employee of an organization producing accessories for the automotive industry, entered the meeting room with his pants completely wet in the front. It looked like he had some issues in the toilet. Since he was late and he had to cross the meeting room, it was impossible for others to not see the problem. Noticing the way his colleagues looked at him, Mr Rastogi said: 'It seems that even birds know that I am a nobody here. I was having lunch in the garden of the company and a bird pooed on my pants. Sorry for the delay, but I had to remove "the gift". I hope I do not stink!' All the participants in the meeting chuckled.

Negotiation

Negotiation is very common in work settings. Negotiation can be related to prices, quantities, competing ideas, resource allocation, contract definition etc.

Humour can be used during negotiations in order to establish a positive atmosphere since the beginning, change the counterpart's perspective during the bargaining, transfer information which is otherwise difficult to communicate, and take a step back when the agreement becomes hard to reach.

The use of humour in negotiation is not simply a matter of telling jokes, but involves the expression of spontaneous humour in the flow of conversation to alter perspectives, change disabling expectations, reframe relationships, and provide multiple points of view on the topic.

In addition, using appropriate humour increases the likeability of a communicator and liked communicators have more influential power than the disliked ones. Thus, during a negotiation, a humorous person maybe more effective due to his attractive communication skills and, in turn, his influential power. Humour also influences the perceived importance of the object of the negotiation. For example, a joke may communicate that the other person is not taking the situation very seriously and this behaviour may make people less averse to concessions because the situation becomes less important than previously thought.

It has been studied that during negotiation activities, subjects who received a demand accompanied by humour made a greater concession than non-humour demands. Terry Kurtzberg and some other researchers, for example, conducted 2 studies involving executive MBA students in order to investigate the role of humour in online negotiations. The first study demonstrated that starting a negotiation by email with humour resulted in higher trust and satisfaction, higher joint gains for the negotiating couple, and also higher individual gains for the party that first used humour. The second study found that first proposals in distributive negotiation fall more frequently within the bargaining zone when online negotiations begin with humour, and that the final gains of negotiations occurring within a humorous framework were also more equally distributed between the counterparties compared to e-transactions without a humorous start.

Negotiation: Strange offer

The Head of the Purchase Department and the Chief Information Officer of the company XYZ called Mrs Mehta, the Key Account Manager of an IT consultancy company, to discuss the renewal of their contract. The contract was fixed-price and it consisted of a number of pre-defined days of support.

Head of Purchase Department: 'After 2 years of collaboration we were able to monitor the usage of your service and we discovered that we are using lesser days than those mentioned in the contract. We understand that this is not your fault but this is an issue. In addition, we have come across market suppliers that offer the same service at a lower price.'

Key Account Manager: 'I do not know what kind of suppliers you are referring to but the quality of our personnel is very high, we are speaking about mission critical components of your IT infrastructure, it would be very risky to put in the hands of a junior personnel this kind of service. I am sorry if you do not use all the days available in the contract, but from our side, since we guarantee our intervention in a few hours, we cannot assign the same employee to other tasks, so for us the low usage is not a factor that increases our profitability.'

CIO: 'I understand, but still the service is too expensive, we have to cut costs and so you have to reduce the value of the contract, of course if you are still interested in working with us.'

The situation was not the best and the Key Account Manager knew that cutting more than 25 per cent of the value of the contract would result in losing money.

Key Account Manager: 'Of course we are interested in continuing work with you. I guess you feel the same since from the feedback you gave us you appear to be very satisfied with our service.'

Head of Purchase Department: 'It is not a question of satisfaction, it is a question of costs!'

Key Account Manager: 'To show you that we really care about our business relationship, we can cut the value of the contract by 5 per cent.'

Head of Purchase Department: 'Sorry, we are not on the right track. We were thinking more at 30 per cent.'

The situation was really bad. 30 per cent was too much.

Key Account Manager: 'If, without any further yearly review, you sign the contract for 3 years, I can arrive to 10 per cent, honestly 30 per cent is not feasible.'

Head of Purchase Department: 'Okay 3 years, but 25 per cent discount.'

Key Account Manager: 'Let us go for 25 per cent only if it is 3 years plus my 3 sons and my dog!'

Head of Purchase Department: 'Sorry?'

Key Account Manager: 'At 25 per cent I would have no money to feed my family! You will love them!'

The Head of Purchase Department and the CIO laughed. In the end, they agreed on a 3-year contract with a 15 per cent discount. The Key Account Manager was quite satisfied.

In this case, the Key Account Manager tried to communicate since the beginning that the requests of the customer were not feasible, but since the negotiation started in a very tough way, it was clear that it would have been almost impossible to conclude the negotiation in a

> satisfactory way. Continuing the negotiation in a serious way would probably end up in a failure (no contract or contract with no profit margin). Therefore, she tried to use another strategy: by adding a humour flavour to the negotiation process, she changed the mindset of the counterparts and she politely communicated that 25 per cent was still impossible. The message arrived loud and clear to the counterparts, without increasing the tension or better, by defusing the tension among parties.

Michael Mulkay and some other researchers recorded sales negotiations in a parts supply company between a salesperson and a potential customer. In this context, humour was used to deal with difficulties during the negotiation process by avoiding direct confrontations and ensuring that neither party felt embarrassed, while still pursuing their goals.

Viveka Adelsward and Britt-Marie Oberg found that during negotiation sessions, humour frequency increased during topic transition (for e.g. from introduction to discussion) in an attempt to structure the negotiation process and to signal the desire to move on to a different topic without appearing to be rude.

Conflict Management

Conflict resolution skills are necessary for almost all the workers to prevent behaviour of other counterparts from degenerating into irreconcilable situations that may prohibit them from working together productively ever again.

It seems that the social-play activity of humour was co-opted over the course of human evolution as a way for people to deal with the multiplicity and inherent contradiction in their communication with one another. By simultaneously expressing opposite meanings, the humorous mode provides a shared conceptual framework that embraces contradictions, rather than avoiding them, and thereby enables people to negotiate otherwise difficult interpersonal transactions. By using humour to joke about each other's perspective, one can communicate a sense of acceptance and appreciation of one another while still maintaining and acknowledging their different points of view.

Conflict can be managed by means of different strategies. Most common are the following ones: avoiding, confronting, smoothing, forcing and compromising. Humour has an impact on each of these strategies.

Humour can be used as an avoidance conflict resolution style. This result can be obtained thanks to the coping function of humour that lowers the emotional involvement related to a situation. Humour can cut the chain of emotions, words and events that create tension and suddenly changes the dominant cognitive perspective.

Avoidance conflict resolution style: You will never believe what happened!

Mr Pathak is a young and very skilled professional, working for a financial service company. He is a high performer but he is unable to arrive on time at the office in the morning. His boss spoke to him many times but almost nothing changed. Five days before, his boss decided to opt for the hard way. He told Mr Pathak that if he would be late once more the following month, he would have him fired.

Mr Pathak understood that it was time to change his behaviour. The first 4 days after the reprimand were fine, but on the fifth day he again forgot to set the alarm clock and arrived 45 minutes late. Before entering in the office, he saw his boss from the glass door, looking at him. He knew that that day could have been his last day in that company. Suddenly, he had a stroke of genius. He ripped a sleeve of his shirt, messed up his hair and started to hobble. He was aware that the boss and the other people saw what he had done. He opened the door and he said: 'You will never believe what happened to me! I was walking on the sidewalk and suddenly a piece of metal hanging from a truck hit me on the left arm and it ripped my sleeve. I tried to run after the truck to warn the driver of the hazards he was causing, but then I fell because I lost a shoe. My leg was injured, but I still decided to walk to office even if it was very painful since I love my job.'

All the other employees were trying to hide their smiles and laughter.

The boss, trying to remain serious, said: 'Okay okay, just start working.'

In this case, Mr Pathak tried to avoid a conflict that would probably lead to very severe consequences. He was aware that the boss was looking at him before entering the door, so he tried to do something so strange and crazy that he was able to interrupt the feeling of anger in his boss. This strategy was not risk free, because it could even worsen the situation. Probably Mr Pathak knew his boss, and he was confident that changing the setting would be much better than opening a serious conversation.

Humour is also linked to the confronting conflict resolution style. Confronting means facing the conflict directly and examining possible solutions. Humour, mostly in the form of metaphors, shows a situation under different perspectives thus permitting people to deal with a broader set of alternatives.

> **Confronting conflict resolution style:
> Pay attention to workaholics**
>
> A meeting among the top managers of a company in the automotive sector:
>
> The top management was mainly composed of two groups: one group that was used to analyse in depth the issues and to use a scientific approach based on studies and data analysis, another group was more keen on using gut feelings as a decision-making tool, thus being less prone to analyse problems in depth.
>
> One of the issues was if the company needed additional workers or not.
>
> Manager 1: 'We do not need new employees, the real problem is that their productivity is too low!'
>
> Manager 2: 'I agree, our people have to be more committed to the company. We cannot just hire, we have to optimize what we have.'
>
> Manager 3: 'I do not agree, our productivity is better than our competitors, we cannot judge productivity based on feelings, we need numbers!'
>
> Manager 2: 'I do not need numbers when facts are so evident! I wish that all of our employees would work like Mr Hisaria. He works from 8.00 a.m. to 10.00 p.m. every

> day. If all the employees were like him, we would need only half of our current workforce!' (Actually, Mr Hisaria worked a lot of hours but he could not be considered a good employee since he did not coordinate with the other employees. He was used to working in isolation and when the other people had to integrate with his outputs, half of the work had to be redone since it was not compliant with what was needed).
>
> Manager 4: 'As NASA suggests: pay attention to workaholics, without proper direction they can do disasters at rates unimaginable for other people!'
>
> Manager 2: 'Good one! Yes, I agree. I do not want that all the people work 15 hours a day, however, it is possible to optimize the current workforce.'
>
> In this case, fourth manager used a well-known sentence that perfectly fitted with the topic and also provided a funny answer. The intent was not to avoid the conflict but to have a confrontation with less tension. It can be noticed that the second manager lowered his tone and was more open to further discussions.

Smoothing conflict management strategy focuses on the relevance of common and shared goals. In this context, humour can be used to augment the positivity of a situation, playing down differences and thus attempting to create a common ground.

Smoothing conflict management style: The strange ingredient

A company working in the consultancy field was deciding the new hiring strategy. The heads of the different departments were involved in the discussion.

Head of Marketing: 'In my opinion, we need more young people because our company hired many senior professionals in the past and now we have a very high average cost. The market is no longer paying us such a big premium price just for the seniority!'

Head of Accounting: 'In my opinion, we need people with a more managerial and organizational background. We have a lot of excellent technicians but we do not have people that excel in customer management.'

Head of Information Systems: 'In my opinion, we need to hire people more committed to our corporate values!'

Head of Marketing: 'I do not agree, they have to be young and low-cost, that is what we need!'

Head of Information Systems: 'Low-cost may also mean low quality, it can be really dangerous investing in low-quality people.'

Head of Marketing: 'I did not say that they have to be low quality!'

Head of Accounting: 'Maybe not but it is a risk, I find your strategy quite risky!'

Head of Human Resources: 'Sorry, I see your requests as different ingredients of a good cake. I did not see anybody asking to put a piece of poo in the cake!'

Head of Accounting (laughing): 'Honestly, if someone wants to put a piece of poo in the cake I am not interested

> in having a single slice!'
>
> Head of Information Systems (laughing): 'Never know, maybe it already happened and you did not notice!'
>
> Head of Marketing (also laughing): 'You are disgusting!'
>
> Head of Human Resources: 'Okay, let us bake a more traditional cake without secret ingredients. Back to our case, we can just look for young people aligned to our corporate values and with economics and organizational background. I do not see any problems.'
>
> In this case, the head of human resources adopted humour based on a metaphor with the addition of vulgar, but quite common, language. Metaphors by themselves are already powerful; in this case it has been overcharged with humour, thus increasing its effectiveness and the ability to remember it and to recall it during other meetings. Imagine the same participants in a different meeting. If someone adds an irrelevant or unfit idea, colleagues might say: 'Are you adding poo to the cake?'

Humour can also be used to convey ambiguous messages. People can use ambiguous humour to say concepts and ideas that, if communicated directly, would offend others. This type of humour permits people to not expose too much themselves and to give the impression that a first step toward the conflict resolution has been made. This use of humour can be related to the compromising conflict resolution style.

Compromising conflict resolution style: It's not your job

Mrs Kedia is a very good software developer but she lacks communication skills. In her company, after 5 years of work experience, software developers are eligible for project management roles. Mrs Kedia would like to be a project manager but, unfortunately her boss communicated to her that she was not selected.

Mrs Kedia said to her boss: 'I know that there were several candidates so I was not sure if I'd be selected for the project manager role but the person selected is the worst software developer among us. Working with him was a pain!'

Her boss: 'That is way I moved him to another position! I tried to save your life!'

Mrs Kedia smiled.

The boss added: 'Now that you are free from constraints, you can even improve your software development skills! He will have nightmares after seeing your performance!'

Mrs Kedia laughed and said: 'Okay, thanks for saving my life. However, is there a possibility of becoming a project manager in the future?'

The boss: 'For now enjoy your new life. then if you are still really interested, we can speak about that.'

Mrs Kedia: 'Okay, thanks.'

In this case, Mrs Kedia's boss used a kind of manipulative approach. He did not tell her that the real problem was her poor communication skills. Thanks to mild humour, he underlined the key competencies and the real future of Mrs Kedia: software development. Even when Mrs Kedia insisted, he created a link with the previous gag (I saved your life) to postpone the decision.

Finally, humour can also be used to force the conflict resolution. In fact, humour can also express hostility and aggressiveness. Embedding aggressive messages in a humorous form is perceived less risky for the sender and less hostile to the receiver but leaves the meaning intact.

> **Forcing conflict resolution style: The coffee machine**
>
> Mr Yadav is employed in a company that builds components for electric transformers. He always complaints of being too busy and stressed. The problem is that he gives these frequent 'speeches' while at the vending machines. The reality is that he is too lazy.
>
> His supervisor assigned him a new project. During the first meeting, as soon as Mr Yadav realized the additional effort required, he said to his supervisor: 'Sorry, but you know that I am already very busy, I do not know if I will be able to manage these additional tasks also.'
>
> The supervisor replied: 'Do not worry, I already found a solution. We are going to move the vending machine closer to your office!'
>
> All the participants laughed.
>
> In this case, the supervisor clearly stated that the real problem was the idle time of Mr Yadav but instead of publicly and directly saying, 'You are lazy and you have to work more!' He used humour to convey the message.
>
> In this situation, Mr Yadav was trapped; he knew that the supervisor was right but he would like to disagree. However, since the communication style was humorous, he knew that replying to humour in a very serious way would result in a tough confrontation or in his supervisor replying: 'I was joking'. In both the cases, he would be the loser.

Conflicts, if properly managed are positive, because they permit people to confront ideas, opinions and knowledge. Not permitting conflicts to come to light can be dangerous, because then tension can rise and people may respond with stress or are pushed to the limits, at which point no negotiations can solve the situation.

It has to be noted that humour does not remove the conflicts but it just shows them in a more acceptable and manageable way.

Leadership

We could say that a good leader should be able to use humour in all the situations depicted above. As a matter of fact, humour is a characteristic often associated with leadership, team effectiveness and leaders' ability to elicit change in subordinates. Humour can be ascribed as one of the characteristics of successful leaders, the others being clever, persuasive, creative and socially skilled. As reported by Diane Brady, journalist at *Bloomberg Businessweek*: 'Indeed, managers of the 21st century need to develop a new set of tools to be successful, and if intelligence, passion and charisma have been and will remain core leadership attributes, future leaders will also need to develop, among other skills, their spontaneity and sense of humour.'

Audrey Pihulyk, author and motivational speaker, opposed authoritarian leaders, calling them intolerant and inflexible to changes. On the contrary, she described humorous leaders as open-minded and less intimidated by changes. According to her, leaders who do not take themselves seriously, but show a humorous approach to their own mistakes and those of their subordinates, are able to create a more relaxed and productive working atmosphere, as they make subordinates feel part of the team and be more effective. Humour is a fundamental trait for leaders. Several successful companies, such as Ben and Jerry's, Southwest Airlines and Sun, have reported higher degrees of employees' commitment, group work cohesiveness and performances to their leader's use of humour. Generally speaking, it emerges that good leaders seem to be humorous (either in the sense of humour initiators or appreciators), whereas bad leaders not. As Mary Crawford noted: 'Perhaps of all the communicative strategies that leaders utilize, the use of humour is most promising, but least understood.'

One of the typical issues when speaking of humour and leadership is that leaders very often fear humour. In fact, they may think that humour is not aligned with their status and using humour may decrease their leadership effectiveness. In a survey filled by more than 2,000 respondents, I asked how a leader that uses humour is considered. Respondents could provide ratings from 1 to 7, where 4 was the neutral value (i.e. no difference between a leader that uses humour and a leader that does not use it). The overall average was 5.18, indicating that generally subordinates prefer leaders that do use humour.

Bruce Avolio, Jane Howell and John Sosik examined the role of humour on leadership styles and subordinates' performances. Results showed that transformational and contingent reward leaders were more likely to use humour, while the opposite was true for laissez-faire leaders.[7] While

---

[7] Laissez-faire is a type of leadership style in which leaders are hands-off and allow group members to make the decisions. Researchers have found this to generally be a leadership style that results in the lowest productivity among group members. Transformational leadership is a style of leadership where the leader collaborates with employees to

there were no clear results with regard to the effect of the use of humour by transformational leaders on individual and group performances, contingent rewards leaders had a negative impact on subordinates' performance when they made more use of humour. This probably happened because subordinates interpreted the use of humour as inconsistent with the seriousness of setting goals and targets. On the contrary, the use of humour by laissez-faire leaders enhanced performances by reducing the negative effects usually associated with their lack of leadership, proving that humour may improve the working environment even when subordinates are dissatisfied with their leader.

Let us assume that humour is an effective managerial tool that could contribute to employees' working effectiveness and satisfaction. In a study, Wayne Decker noted that respondents that rated their supervisor to have a high sense of humour reported higher level of job satisfaction, and judged other supervisor's qualities higher than leaders with a low sense of humour. In general, the differences between ratings, given low and high sense of humour supervisors, were greater for younger (under 25) subjects than older. Older females downgraded supervisors who used sexual humour, while younger females and males did not. In another study, Wayne Decker and Denis Rotondo found that positive humour was associated with positive leaders' perception, while negative humour was associated with negative leaders' association. Decker and

---

identify the needed change, creating a vision to guide the change through inspiration, and executing the change in tandem with committed members of the group. Contingent-reward leadership is a style of leadership that uses recognition and rewards for goals as motivating forces for its members.

Rotondo also found that women bosses who used non-offensive humour were judged as more efficient at getting things done than their less comical counterparts. Moreover, mirthful managers were more likely to be concerned about their staff's well-being. While ratings for male supervisors also rose when they made humour part of their managerial repertoire, men benefited from active funny bones less than women. While self-deprecating and non-offensive humour scored the most points with Decker's respondents, he suggests that managers note what works best in their offices. But whether a supervisor's style is satirical or silly, spontaneous humour and offhand remarks work better than memorized jokes. Decker warned, 'Bosses shouldn't try to be stand-up comedians.'

Kathilyn Philbrick found statistical relationships between humour-initiator respondents (i.e. humour producers) and a task-oriented leadership style (i.e. the leader focuses on the tasks that need to be performed in order to meet certain goals, or to achieve a certain performance standard), and between humour-appreciator respondents and a relationship-oriented leadership attitude (i.e. the leader focuses on the satisfaction, motivation and the general well-being of the team members). Moreover, good leaders generally rated themselves as more humour appreciators rather than humour producers. Differences was also found between male and female respondents, with the former being more equal in number as both initiators and appreciators, and the latter being more often humour appreciators than producers.

Robert Vecchio and some other researchers conducted a study on the use of humour by leaders on their behaviour and subordinates' performances in an educational setting. He found that a leader's use of humour in an educational setting was positively related to subordinates' job performance and enhanced the positive effects of a contingent rewarding leadership style and of leaders' integrity on subordinates' working performance.

Panagiotsi Gkorezis and others investigated the impact of leaders' use of humour on their subordinates' psychological empowerment. Results showed that positive humour, such as affiliative, could ease interpersonal interactions by reducing power distance between leaders and their subordinates, and in turn support employees' empowerment. Accordingly, negative humour was found to impede relationships and motivation. Short-tenure employees reported a stronger correlation between leaders' use of positive humour and psychological empowerment compared to long-tenure ones. Furthermore, leaders' use of negative humour resulted in a higher decrease in the psychological empowerment of long-tenure employees compared to the short-tenure ones.

Another interesting and extensive contribution on humour and leadership is proposed by Susanna Garancini (actually she was one of my students and I am really proud of her!). The first part of the analysis studied subordinates' perceptions of their leaders as humour appreciators and humour initiators. Results showed that male leaders are perceived to produce humour more than women. In addition, it appeared that male leaders were considered more humour initiators than humour producers, and the opposite was found for female leaders.

The analysis also took into consideration the leadership style of the leaders as follows:

- Autocratic, which can be described as: 'My boss provides clear expectations for what needs to be done, when it

should be done, and how it should be done. He/she also sets a clear division between himself/herself and his/her subordinates and makes decisions independently, with little or no input from his/her subordinates.'
- Democratic, which can be summarized as: 'My boss makes the final decisions, but includes his/her subordinates in the decision-making processes, providing guidance to them and encouraging their creativity and engagement in projects and choices.'
- Laissez-faire, which can be explained as: 'My boss offers little or no guidance to his/her subordinates and leaves the decision-making up to them, giving a lot of freedom in how they do their work and how they set their deadlines. He/she provides support with resources and advice if needed, but otherwise he/she doesn't get involved.'

It emerged that democratic leaders tend to also be humour appreciators, laissez-faire leaders are humour appreciators too, but less than democratic leaders, while autocratic leaders are the least humour appreciators. Similar results, but smaller in absolute terms, have been found between leadership styles and humour production.

The second part of the study carried out by Garancini investigated the frequency with which leaders generally employ humour at work. Results indicated that leaders use humour in the workplace with a moderate frequency and that male leaders use humour more frequently than female ones.

In particular, male subordinates evaluating male leaders reported the highest frequency, followed by female respondents reporting male leaders, men rating women, and female-female couples. In terms of leadership styles democratic leaders use humour more often than laissez-faire leaders while autocratic leaders are the ones that use humour with the lowest frequency. The effect of use of humour on leaders' authority was also studied. As already suggested by other studies, results confirmed that humour does not undermine leaders' authority, but on the contrary helps to improve subordinates' opinion on leaders.

The third part investigated the use of humour by leaders in specific circumstances or for a particular purpose. Results are summarized below.

Occasions of Use of Humour by Leaders

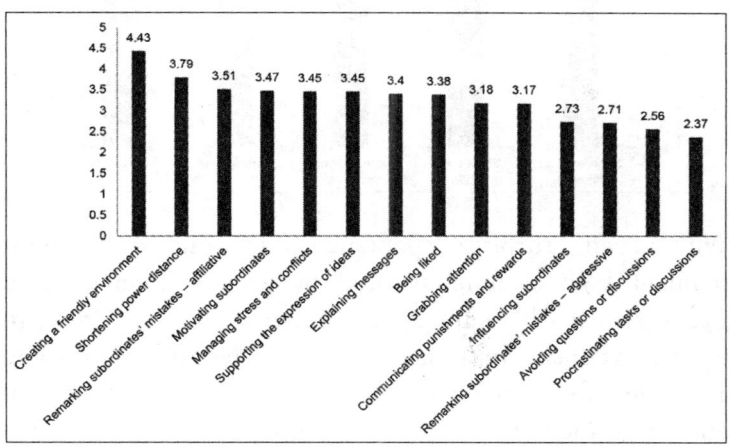

It can be noticed that the first goal is quite general in purpose, in fact, leaders use humour in an attempt to create a friendly environment. It is also interesting to notice that humour is used to correct/remark the mistakes made by subordinates but in a benign way. Humour is thus used as a non-threatening way to correct unwanted behaviour. Even with minor frequency, it can be noted that leaders sometimes use humour as an 'escaping' mechanism to avoid questions or discussions or to procrastinate task execution.

Garancini also analysed the origin of leaders' humour (see below).

Types of Humour Used by Leaders

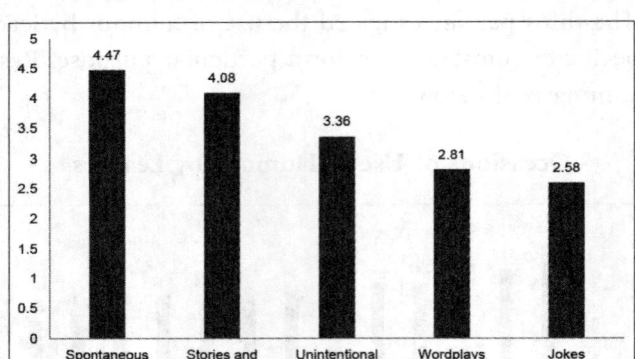

Without any surprise, spontaneous humour is the most frequent type of humour used by leaders. Interesting to notice also the high frequency of stories and anecdotes. In the management and communication literature stories and anecdotes are considered very powerful tools. In fact, on one hand, they are very useful to grab the attention of the audience; on the other hand, they also show that persons telling (interesting) stories are seen as having interesting lives thus increasing their leadership status.

Adding more details, male leaders use all the considered forms of humour more frequently than female ones. In terms of leadership styles, autocratic leaders use all the humour types with less frequency compared to lassez-faire and democratic leaders.

Finally, Garancini also studied what was the topic addressed with humour.

Humour Content

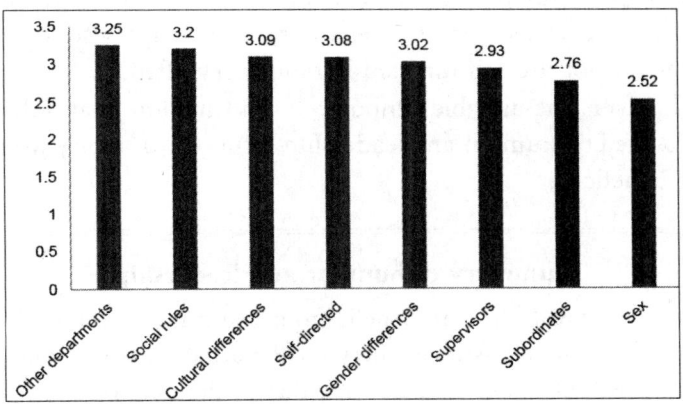

As far as humour content is concerned, the leaders' most and least recurrent humour subjects are humour in other departments and humour in religion respectively. Given that religion is a very sensitive topic, the low frequency of humour in religion can be considered good news. It is a quite interesting fact that humour in other departments is the most used kind of humour. Humour often flourishes more when differences are noted, meaning that people working in different departments are different in their behaviour. From a managerial perspective, this is not good, since it means that functional boundaries are still strong in many organizations. Speaking about gender, men choose sexual humour, humour on social rules, on cultural differences and religious humour more frequently than women do, thus indicating and confirming that they use more aggressive humour than women do. In terms of leadership styles, laissez-faire leaders use humour with less frequency on subordinates, in other departments and self-directed humour. Democratic leaders tend to prefer humour on social rules and self-directed humour more, while trying to limit the usage of humour on subordinates, supervisors and in other departments. Autocratic leaders tend to prefer humour on supervisors while they do not use self-directed humour very often.

Given the notable amount of information that I have provided on humour and leadership, I guess a summary would be beneficial.

Summary of humour and leadership

- Normally leaders benefit from using humour but if you are an asshole (sorry for the artistic license) you will be considered just like that in the long run.
- Using humour benefits more female leaders than male leaders.
- Leaders who use humour also improve the performance of their subordinates.
- If your leadership style is very focused on achieving goals and performing tasks, humour can still play a role but the dosage is fundamental. If used too much, it might be perceived as not aligned with your directions.
- Democratic leaders are the most funniest.
- Male leaders are more humour initiators than appreciators.
- Female leaders are more humour appreciators than initiators.
- Female subordinates share a laugh more often with male leaders than they do with female leaders.

The Dark Side of Humour at the Workplace

In the previous pages, I highlighted the role that humour may have at the workplace. Mostly, I have described positive effects, but a few negative effects have been noticed as well. Unfortunately, there is a narrow gap between the use and abuse of humour. Crossing the fine line may cause one to abuse humour. This implies that some people instead of enjoying humour may fear it. Dr Micheal Titze introduced the term 'gelotophobia' in 1996, after verifying cases of fear-related humour from his personal social contacts. In simple words, the definition of gelotophobia is—the fear of being laughed at. The formation of this term came about from the word 'gelos' and 'phobia' which mean laughter and fear respectively. It is seen as a type of social phobia and has been a study of interest in recent years. Furthermore, gelotophobia results from the menacing effect of frightening someone by laughing at them along with others. This can create serious disturbances and hence, affecting the closeness and intimacy of their social relationship.

Gelotophobia is not so uncommon. On average, 33 per cent of young Indians have some fear of being laughed at. Interestingly, there is almost no difference between men and women in this regard.

Gelotophobia Among Young Indians

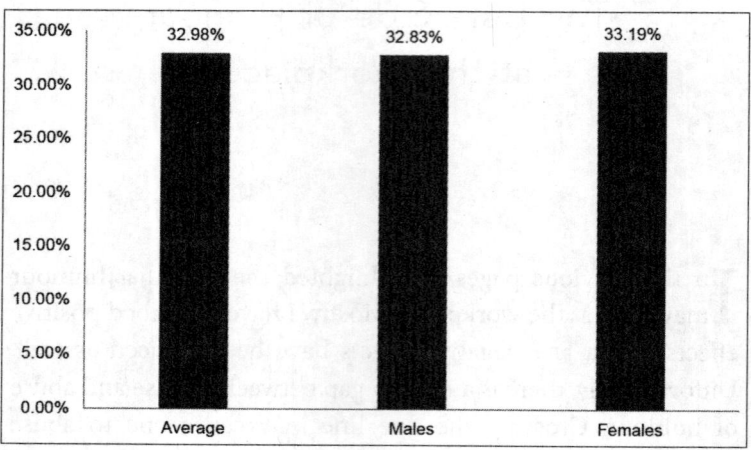

Source: Hiranandani, 2010.

We have all seen situations where humour alienates people and creates barriers. The problem here, of course, is the kind of humour employees use on the job. Humour that disrupts and weakens teams is generally some kind of put-down humour, it is humour in which there is a clear victim or a butt of the joke. This kind of humour always feels like 'laughing at' rather than 'laughing with'. It seems to be part of human nature to tell jokes that poke fun at other groups or individuals.

If you know a lot of jokes and poke fun at other racial or ethnic groups, opposite sex, etc., and tell them on the job, it is just a matter of time until you seriously offend someone (even if they laugh at your joke). With increasing levels of cultural diversity emerging in most work settings, the best rule of thumb is to simply not use any put-down humour on the job. Humour, which you assume will not offend your listeners, can easily offend someone within the earshot of the joke, even though you are not telling it to that person. The one exception to this rule is that it is generally fine to tell jokes putting down your company's main competitors.

Those who love put-down kind of humour, they complain that the workplace has just become too sensitive, and that those who are offended by their jokes need to 'lighten up' a bit. The joke-teller generally says something like, 'Hey, it's just a joke. I was only kidding. What's the matter, can't you take a joke?' The only problem is that unless you know the person telling the joke very well, you can never be sure whether the joke does or does not say something about their true underlying attitude towards whom the joke is aimed at. There are enough people who hold hostile attitude towards the groups they put down in their jokes, so much so that anyone who does not know you well will assume that you fall in this category. Since this can only disrupt the effectiveness with which you work together, the best approach is clearly to find another way to show your sense of humour on the job.

Humour directed at colleagues, mostly about their imperfections, also leaves the audience with a bitter aftertaste. This is due to conflicting signals. Is he/she using humour to defend against his/her own insecurities? Is he/she covering up his/her own fears and pains? Is he/she using making fun of others to mask his/her hostility? Or is he/she (by making others the butt of their jokes) deflecting attention from him/herself, to avoid getting too close to people?

> **Negative humour: You are the right person!**
>
> An employee of a consultancy company was walking along the corridor of the company.
>
> His supervisor approached him and said: 'Right in time, I was looking for you. I decided to assign you the new CRM project.'
>
> He replied: 'Why me?'
>
> His supervisor (laughing): 'Because all the good people are already busy!'
>
> In this case, both laughed, but without additional explanations the employee might either believe that it was only a joke or he might also suspect that some meaning was hidden behind the joke.

In general, sarcastic or derisive humour is often contemptuous, hostile and manipulative. This type of humour reveals more about the person who is attacking rather than the person under attack. Although often disguised as humour, sarcasm is really a thinly disguised form of hostility. It shows a lack of respect for the subject and can be hurtful.

Another questionable implementation of workplace humour is when employees put 'funny notices/cartoons' on the office walls/furniture of their offices/cubicles and it can be accessed by other colleagues or, even worse, by customers. The problem is that those cartoons may be funny for the employee but they can offensive for other people since, very often, they target them. One can say that they act as stress busters for the person who proposed them, but it has been observed that after a few days they are considered part of the background—the employee does not notice their existence anymore, but other people do!

> **Negative side of humour: Funny notice?**
>
> In a cubicle, I saw a notice with these contents:
>
> Office Time Table
>
> | | | |
> |---|---|---|
> | 9 a.m. | – | Starting time |
> | 9.30 a.m. | – | Arriving time |
> | 9.45 a.m. | – | Tea break |
> | 11 a.m. | – | Check email |
> | 11.15 a.m. | – | Prepare for lunch |
> | 12 p.m. | – | Lunch |
> | 2.45 p.m. | – | Browse internet |
> | 3 p.m. | – | Snack time |
> | 4 p.m. | – | Check email |
> | 4.30 p.m. | – | Prepare to go home |
> | 5 p.m. | – | Go home |
>
> While this notice can be funny for the person who puts it up on the wall, I guess his/her boss does not have exactly the same opinion. In addition, the notice could also be seen by customers who had to pass along the corridor, in order to reach a meeting room. In this case, the 'funny' notice also had negative impact on the company image.

> **Negative side of humour: Good customer service?**
>
> This happened to me. An employee of the customer service had a note stuck to the wall with the following phrase:
>
> 'Never argue with stupid people, they will drag you down to their level and then beat you with experience. —Mark Twain.'
>
> Maybe she thought it was funny but since she worked in customer service, I supposed the note was related to the way she considered customers.

Working in International Environments with Humour

Humour is a universal human phenomenon, present in both tribal and industrialized societies. In most societies, there are roles or positions that allow people to joke, or which require a display of humour such as the role of a fool or clown. Moreover, the humour-producing techniques popular in the East are also used in the West. They include exaggeration, invective, understatement, witty cynicism, unexpected twists of logic, verbal irony, disguise, and deception, as well as the appeal to the reader's superiority over victims of small misfortunes.

Theoretically, there is no reason to assume differences in basic cognitive or physiological processes of humour mechanisms across cultures. All cultures laugh and smile at incongruities and their solutions; mechanisms such as surprise, superiority, and tension relief are universal. However, cultural preferences may affect both the specific content and the perception of incongruities and their resolutions, as well as the interpretation of the surprise element. Each culture has its own set of values, norms and unwritten rules of what is appropriate in humour, and these largely determine its content, target and style.

Being humour effective in a multicultural setting is not an easy task. The first issue is language proficiency: in an international team a common known language is used to interact, but the ability to express concepts and ideas in the common language may vary from person to person, thus the ability to convey and appreciate humour can vary too. The second issue is the knowledge of the foreign culture(s). As introduced before, culture plays an important role in humour, what is funny in a given culture may not be funny or may even be offensive in another.

Mahadev Apte addressed the interrelation between culture, communication and humour in his book, *Humour and Laughter: An Anthropological Approach*. First, he explained that communication and humour are interdependent in 2 important ways: (i) language itself becomes the subject matter of humour; (ii) the use and function of language and the cultural attitudes and values associated with it influence the occurrence, comprehension and appreciation of humour. Apte further explained that three factors reflect the cultural bases of humour and are necessary for its development: (i) shared cultural knowledge, (ii) shared rules for interpreting it and (iii) agreement on the cultural appropriateness of the incongruity and exaggeration involved.

Regarding the first issue, John Robert Schmitz addressed the problem of using humour in foreign language courses. He found that the more foreign language students understood a new language, the more different jokes can be cracked in that language. At a basic level, smart answers or retorts to questions or statements can be presented, at a higher level linguistic or word-based humour can be used. Language proficiency should be matched with foreign cultural knowledge, because even a joke made with a basic vocabulary can present culture specific aspects. Taking into consideration these factors is very difficult because a non-sensitive subject in a culture can be very sensitive in another.

Many companies work in an international environment: depending on the organization, customers, colleagues, partners, suppliers etc., might be from different countries. Humour, if used correctly, can be of great value in helping cement multi-cultural teams. It was Victor Borge[8] who said that: 'Humour is the shortest distance between two people.' Humour can be used as a means of airing cultural differences in an informal, non-threatening way. Furthermore, the amount of shared humour within the team can often be used as a yardstick for its cohesiveness. At best, humour can be used to defuse a tense situation or to break the ice. However, humour can be a double-edged sword and should always be used with care and sensitivity to cultural differences.

Patricia Castell and Jeffrey Goldstein compared the content of jokes preferred by students from Belgium, Hong Kong and the United States, and found that US students, unlike the other national groups, preferred jokes with sexual and aggressive content.

Willibald Ruch performed a series of cross-cultural comparisons using a series of jokes and cartoons (the Three

---

[8]Victor Borge (1909–2000), world-class musician and humorist, was pronounced 'the funniest man in the world' by the *New York Times*.

Wit Dimensions or 3WD) and found that people of different nationalities (German, French, British, American, Turkish and Israeli) responded to the same dimensions of humour in a similar way. The first dimension includes a preference for jokes that present incongruities and their resolution. The second dimension is a preference for jokes and cartoons that present incongruities without complete resolution. The third dimension is a preference for jokes and cartoons with sexual content. While the intrinsic structure of the 3WD was stable across nationalities, differences were detected regarding preference for a specific dimension. For example, Italians and Israelis exhibited a significantly stronger preference for jokes and cartoons with sexual content.

While culture can explain some humour preferences, belonging to a specific cultural group is not sufficient in order to explain the response a person may have to jokes about that specific group. Russell Middleton, a professor of sociology, noticed that, even if black people appreciated more—compared to white people—jokes about white people, the two groups do not present different levels of appreciation for anti-blacks jokes. It seems that even people belonging to a specific group may share opinions against the group itself.

In order to delve deeper into this subject, I did an extensive study (2020 valid questionnaires) from 2006 to 2010, then published in 2013. The idea was to study the type of humour used in national and international work settings.

The first question I tried to provide an answer to was: Is it easy to be humorous in an international business environment compared to a national one?

The answers can be seen below. Answers were provided on a scale of 1 to 7 (1 being very difficult and 7 very easy).

Ability to Be Humorous in National versus International Business Environments

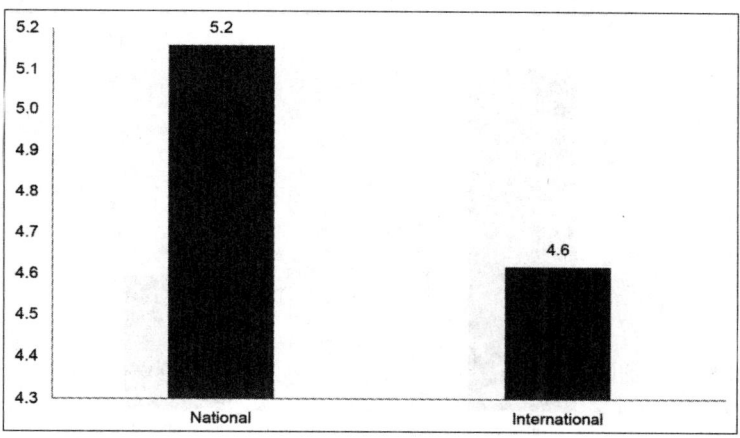

Source: Sampietro, 2013

It appears from the above graph that international business environments pose some challenges to the ability to be humorous. This can be due to the usage of a different language but especially due to culture differences which reduce humour options.

The same can be said for the ability to understand humour in international business environments compared to national ones.

Ability to Understand Humour in National versus International Business Environments

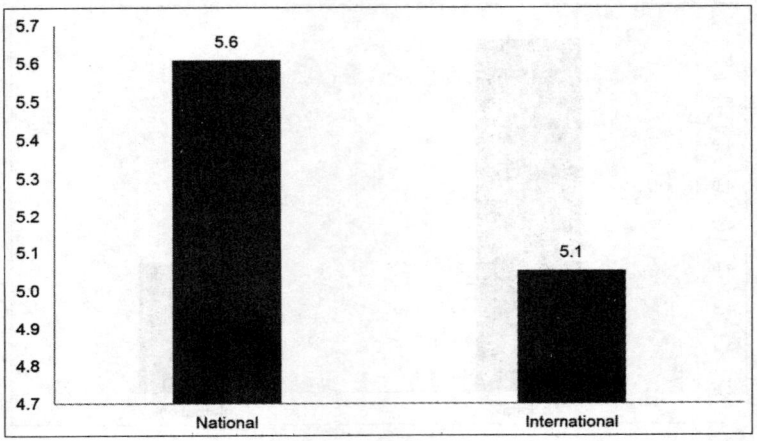

Source: Sampietro, 2013

It has then been studied the type of humour used both in national and international work environments.

The questionnaire for this proposed 11 different humour types. When the international variable was introduced, results showed a generalized 'lowering effect'. It does not mean that international environments are not funny, it is just that some types of humour are used with less frequency.

Humour Types in National versus International Business Environments

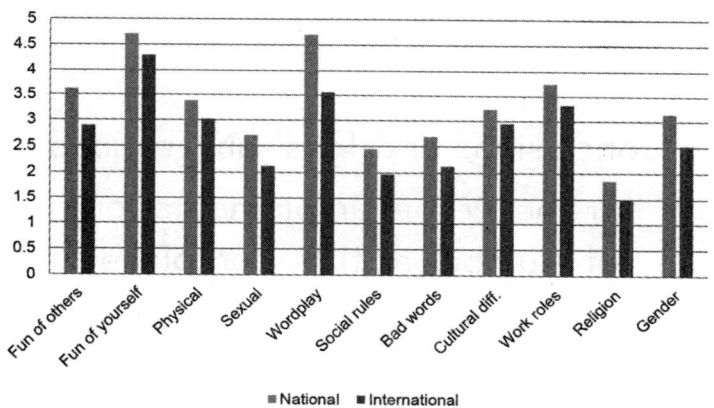

Source: Sampietro, 2013

Collected data does not support the idea that the above mentioned lowering effect is due to English proficiency (the only exception is wordplay humour type), thus it is more probable that people pay more attention in environments where the perceived diversity among team members is considered higher than in national environments and thus, some humour types may not be very welcome.

Conclusions and Final Suggestions for the Proper Implementation of Humour at the Workplace

It would be really a pity leaving humour outside the companies' boundaries. This is not because working is boring and humour is fun, or because the more time we invest in humour the less we work. The actual reason is very simple: humour is almost a part of our lives from our day 1. Humour is natural; it is beneficial from a cognitive development perspective and has positive physical outcomes too (but if you laugh too much you might suffer from syncope, cardiac or oesophageal rupture, protrusion of abdominal hernias, asthma attacks, interlobular emphysema, cataplexy, headaches, jaw dislocation and incontinence).

An ingredient so precious cannot simply be denied or restrained in the business environment because someone has the feeling that it may be harmful for companies' performance.

Anecdotal and scientific evidences suggest that humour, if properly used, has positive effects on personal, team and company performance. This book presented many of those evidences.

If, after having read this book, you agree that companies should find room for humour, the next step is to define a strategy to leverage it.

Unfortunately, you cannot **buy** humour. You cannot go to the supermarket and ask for **a certa**in amount and quality of humour. There are not magic **formulas** to leverage humour at the workplace, however, there are some steps and behaviours that may support positive humour at the workplace.

At the very basic level you can just start tolerating humour (only, of course, if you did not before). It is natural, it is part of human nature and it tells you a lot of interesting things that are going on in your company. If you do not sanction humour (you can if people just laugh and do not work) and at least you just reply with a smile (it is not mandatory to be humour producers, very often leaders are just humour appreciators), people will feel free to use it. In general, being free to use humour will improve the employee morale, but another important outcome is that if you listen to humour exchanges, you can collect valuable information related to your company, department, team, etc. For example:

- You can understand what is going wrong in the company. Humour, in fact, very often is based on situations we do not like. We get rid of those situations just to lower our stress.
- You can understand why some colleagues are disliked, for the same reason as above.
- You can understand the morale of your employees. If the mood is really bad, humour does not flourish or

if it does then it is mostly aggressive.
- You can understand the social relationships in the organization. Normally, we share a laugh with people we like.
- Regardless of the organizational chart, you can understand who has the real power by monitoring humour as ingratiation strategy and the direction that humour takes (top down, bottom up or among peers).

Another action is to recruit people by also taking into consideration their ability to use humour. Humorous people contribute in creating a healthy work environment, they can boost creativity and, more importantly in a competitive environment they are more resilient to stress. Remember that humour is a powerful copying mechanism, and people who have it are better able to face difficult situations.

However, what I really advise against is to implement fake and ridiculous humour strategies. I know that what I am going to say may hurt some humour consultants (yes, there are humour consultants).

On the web, you will find many suggestions to improve humour at the workplace; honestly, I do not like any of them. For a very simple reason: the best humour is spontaneous and situational, there is limited room to engineer it.[9] The best thing you can do is to create an environment where good humour can flourish. Canned or planned humour, such as telling jokes, sticking funny cartoons on the walls, giving nicknames to

---

[9]Humour can be engineered if you are a professional in the humour field (comic actor, comic book writer etc.). But in those cases the scenario is completely different: people are expecting to have fun with you and so you have to be prepared for that.

colleagues, playing stupid games to socialize (sorry, but I hate games that have the open purpose to make you laugh) might have a moderate positive effect if you already work in a positive and funny atmosphere. I once saw on Facebook some pictures of my former students going to work at Google in their pyjamas. The reaction to initiatives like this might be positive in companies where people already have fun but if you work in a company where the organizational climate is very bad, these planned initiatives can really bother employees. In fact, they might be considered not aligned with the dominant mood and even manipulative. The subtle message of these initiatives is: as a company, we only deciding/imposing when and how you should have fun. Great, isn't it? Do you remember the reversal theory of humour? If you are in telic mode, you are not ready to have fun.

Let's now forget very bad organizations and people, instead let's consider normal people who want to improve their humour skills at the workplace.

As I already mentioned, the first step is to welcome humour. However, maybe someone would like to go a step further, that is, learn to be humorous. Again, some humour trainers will not enjoy what I am saying (yes, there are humour trainers as well). Unfortunately, spontaneous humour is very difficult to learn. When it comes to improving inner cognitive abilities, based on genetic and also on many experiences that shape our brain, you can slightly improve them but you cannot completely alter them. If it were possible, everyone would have an IQ of 200! However, some improvements are still possible.

At the very basic level, you can learn a lot of jokes. However, as already pointed out in this book, jokes are not told very often in real settings. In addition, if you do not have humour skills, it is very probable that your jokes will be told in a way that is not funny. As a matter of fact, voice tone, body language and timing, all play a role in the way humour is perceived. If your ability to tell jokes is good, increasing the available number in your memory is not a bad idea since you will be ready to use them in many circumstances. In addition, looking for jokes has a spillover effect: they may improve your mood and we know that positive emotions elicit a more intense use of humour. However, it has to be clear that just knowing more jokes does not have a huge impact on your humour rating.

As mentioned in the leadership paragraph, a quite common and effective way to be humorous is to tell stories and anecdotes. They are far better than jokes since they are perceived as more spontaneous. In particular, they work very well if they are based on personal experiences. In fact, if personal experience is embedded in stories and anecdotes, you are telling something about yourself to your counterparts. In this way, you are reducing the emotional distance and creating more connections with your audience. The good thing about stories and anecdotes is that they can be planned, that is, you can try to collect them, to shape them in a humorous way and to test them.

The above strategy is not risk free. In fact:

- Stories and anecdotes normally are limited in number. That means that if you are exposed to the same people, there is a high risk that you are going to repeat the same stories and anecdotes more than once to them, and that is not funny.
- They have to be linked to a specific conversational

context. Normally, you do not start a conversation with a story or anecdote; most probably you use them to engage in an ongoing conversation. You cannot just jump-in a conversation with a story not linked with the conversation content.

- They have to be aligned to the audience culture, social context and economic conditions of the audience. For example, imagine a group of subordinates sharing a laugh on the fact that one of them stained the seat of his/her car because of a chocolate bar in his/her pocket. If subordinates have a Tata Nano and you own a Ferrari, you cannot enter in the discussion and say: 'Oh, it happened to me as well but the chocolate was so much that when I parked the Ferrari people thought it was poop! Finally, I had to change the seat! It cost more than 10 lakh!' This story can be funny if shared with other rich people, but if shared with people who can only dream of a Ferrari, it can be considered impolite and just a way to show that you are better than them.

Unfortunately, the best way to be humorous, which is being able to produce spontaneous and situational humour, is the most difficult to improve. As I mentioned before, here we deal with our inner characteristics, not with technical skills, which are easier to learn. In addition, humour is not only based on contents, also the envelope is fundamental (voice, body language, timing, etc.). Maybe some very good humour trainers exist in the world, so my advice may not be representative of the state-of-the-art in humour development. Yet, here are some suggestions:

- Observe humorous people. As in every observational

activity, when you observe you will also be influenced by the subject observed. In this way, even without noticing, you will increase your natural humour skills.
- Stay with humorous people. It is difficult to develop your humour skills if you normally invest your time with non-humorous people.
- Invest your time in humorous activities such as watching comic films, reading funny books, going to comic theatre shows. Again, if your sole hobby is watching videos of wars and natural disasters, probably your humour skills will not receive a boost.
- Observe the reactions to your humorous stimuli. This is very important. Sometimes you may have the wrong perception that you are not humorous while in practice you are. On the opposite, sometimes you might overestimate your humorous skills. Noticing feedbacks can really fine-tune your humour style and make it better. However, in social contexts, very often people react with fake smiles instead of not laughing at all. So that, you have to be able to distinguish between a genuine smile and a fake one (see the box below for details).

How to distinguish between a real and a fake smile

First of all, faking a smile is not always bad, even a plastered smile can sometimes be better that nothing. Sometimes you just fake a smile because you did not understand a humorous exchange and you do not want to appear dumb or be socially isolated. On an average, 40 per cent of the people are not able to recognize a fake smile. This percentage is based on visual experiments, that is, people were told to observe faces of smiling people and report when the smile of genuine or fake. Since in real life we do not pay much attention as in a test, we can expect that very often fake smiles are not detected.

The science behind detecting real smiles started with Guillaume Duchenne (1806–1875), a famous French physician. He decided to test it out in a rather extreme fashion. He was interested in the muscles that are involved in creating facial expressions, which he believed were associated with specific emotions.

To test his hypothesis he attached electrodes to the skin near facial muscles and then he run current through them.

He discovered the muscles' group involved in many facial expressions, one of them is the genuine smile, also known today as the 'Duchenne', named after its discoverer.

He discovered that any real smile leverages:

- Orbicularis Oris, which is the muscle that pulls away the lips and creates the familiar stretch on the face.
- Zygomatic Major, which is normally activated in genuine smiles only. This muscle creates the small cringes around our eyes and nose when we smile.

The main tip is: when you look at a smiling face, look at the eyes, if they 'smile' as well then it is a good sign. If you do not see any change, it is a strong sign that they are faking it. However, with practice it is possible to create fake smiles that seem genuine.

Fortunately, there are some other good indicators:

- How fast the smile appears. Genuine smiles are late-coming; they don't appear instantly on demand.
- How often and long it stays. Real smiles appear in succession and last somewhat longer.
- How big and symmetrical they are. It might sound counter-intuitive but real smiles are not that big and they are not always symmetrical. When we do fake a smile we want to really show it, so we often overstretch it because we believe that real smiles are big and symmetrical, but they are not.

To conclude, I hope I was able to give you a better understanding of a complex and currently underestimated topic such as humour at the workplace. Humour, if properly used, can be a powerful ally to performance at all levels (individual, team, department or a company). Just try. In the worst-case scenario, you simply had fun.

Bibliography

Abel M.H., Maxwell D., 'Humour and Affective Consequences of a Stressful Task', *Journal of Social & Clinical Psychology*, 2002, Vol. 21 Issue 2, pp. 165–90.

Abramis D.J., 'Humour in Healthy Organizations', *HR Magazine*, 1992, Vol. 37 No. 8.

Adelsward V., OBERG B., 'The Function of Laughter and Joking in Negotiation Activities', *Humour—International Journal of Humour Research*, 1998, Vol. 11 Issue 4, pp. 411–29.

Alderfer C., *Existence, Relatedness, and Growth*, Free Press, 1972.

Anonimous, 'The Sense of Joy', *Nation*, 1927, p. 124.

Apte M.L., *Humour and Laughter: An Anthropological Approach*, Cornell University Press, 1985.

Apter M.J., *The Experience of Motivation: The Theory of Psychological Reversals*, Academic Press, 1982.

Apter M.J., *A Structural-Phenomenology of Play*, Swets & Zeitlinger, 1991.

Apter M.J., KERR J.H., (Eds.), *Adult Play: A Reversal Theory Approach*, Swets & Zeitlinger, 1991, pp. 13–29.

Apter M.J. (Ed.), *Motivational Styles in Everyday Life: A Guide to Reversal Theory*, American Psychological Association, 2001.

Autissier D., Arnèguy È., *Petittraitè de l'humour au travail*, Eyrolles, 2012.

Avolio B.J., Howell J.M., Sosik J.J., 'A Funny Thing Happened on the

Way to the Bottom Line: Humour as a Moderator of Leadership Style Effects', *The Academy of Management Journal*, Academy of Management, Vol. 42 Issue 2, pp. 219–27.

Barlett M.S., 'A Note on the Multiplying Factors for Various Chi Square Approximations', *Journal of the Royal Statistical Society*, 1954, 16, pp. 296–98.

Baron R.A., Ball R.L., 'The Aggression-Inhibiting Influence of Nonhostile Humor', *Journal of Experimental Social Psychology*, 1974, 10(1), pp. 23–33.

Baron R.A., 'Aggression-Inhibiting Influence of Sexual Humor', *Journal of Personality & Social Psychology*, 1978a, 36(2), pp. 189–97.

Baron R.A., 'The Influence of Hostile and Nonhostile Humor Upon Physical Aggression', *Personality & Social Psychology Bulletin*, 1978b, 4(1), pp. 77–80.

Barreca R., *They Used to Call Me Snow White…but I Drifted: Women's Strategic Use of Humour*, Penguin Books, 1991.

Bass B., *Bass & Stogdill's Handbook of Leadership*, 3rd Ed., Free Press, 1990.

Bell N.D., 'How Native and Non-Native English Speakers Adapt to Humour in Intercultural Interaction', *Humour–International Journal of Humour Research*, 2007, 20(1), pp. 27–48.

Bergen D., *Development of the Sense of Humour*, in RUCH W.(Ed.), *The Sense of Humour: Explorations of a Personality Characteristic*, Berlin, Walter de Gruyter, 1998a, pp. 329–58.

Bergen D., *Play as a Context for Humour Development*, in Fromberg D.P., Bergen D.(Eds.), *Play from Birth to Twelve and Beyond: Contexts, Perspectives, and Meanings*, New York, Garland, 1998b, pp. 324–37.

Berger A.A., 'Anatomy of the Joke', *Journal of Communication*, 1976, 26, pp. 113–15.

Berk L.S., Tan S.A., Fry W.F., Napier B.J., Lee J.W., Hubbard R.W., et al., 'Neuroendocrine and Stress Hormone Changes During Mirthful Laughter', *American Journal of the Medical Sciences*, 1989, 298, pp. 390–96.

Berkowitz L., 'Aggressive Humour as a Stimulus to Aggressive Responses', *Journal of Personality & Social Psychology*, 1970, 16(4), pp. 710–17.

Berlyne D.E., *Conflict, Arousal, and Curiosity*, McGraw-Hill, 1960.

Berlyne D.E., *Laughter, Humour, and Play*, in Lindzey G., Aronson E.(Eds.), *The Handbook of Social Psychology*, 2nd Ed., Reading, Addison-Wesley, 1969, Vol. 3, pp. 795–852.

Berlyne D.E., *Humour and its Kin*, in Goldstein J.H., Mcghee P. E.(Eds.), *The Psychology of Humour: Theoretical Perspectives and Empirical Issues*, Academic Press, 1972, pp. 43–60.

Besemer S.P., Treffinger, D.J., 'Analysis of Creative Products: Review and Synthesis', *Journal of Creative Behavior*, 1981, 15, pp. 158–78.

Blake R., Mouton J., *The Managerial Grid: The Key to Leadership Excellence*, Gulf Publishing Co., 1964.

Bower T.G.R., 'The Object in the World of the Infant', *Scientific American*, 1971, 225, pp. 30–38.

Bower T.G.R., *Development in Infancy*, Freeman, 1974.

Brady D., 'Wanted: Eclectic Visionary with a Sense of Humour', *Business Week*, August 28, 2000, 143–44.

Brown R.B., Keegan D., 'Humour in the Hotel Kitchen', *Humour: International Journal of Humour Research*, 1999, 12(1), pp. 47–70.

Bryant J., *Degree of Hostility in Squelches as a Factor in Humour Appreciation*, in Chapman A.J., Foot H.C.(Eds.), *It's a Funny Thing, Humour*, Oxford, Pergamon Press, 1977, pp. 321–27.

Burchell B., Marsh C., 'The Effect of Questionnaire Length on Survey Response', *Quality & Quantity*, 1992, 26(3), pp. 233–44.

Byrne D., 'The Relationship between Humour and the Expression of Hostility', *Journal of Abnormal & Social Psychology*, 1956, 53, pp. 84–89.

Cann A., Calhoun L.G., Banks J.S., 'On the Role of Humour Appreciation in Interpersonal Attraction: It's No Joking Matter', *Humour— International Journal of Humour Research*, 1997, 10(1), pp. 77–89.

Cann A., Holt K., Calhoun L.G., 'The Roles of Humour and Sense of Humour in Responses to Stressors', *Humour—International Journal of Humour Research*, 1999, 12(2), pp. 177–93.

Cantor J.R., 'What is Funny to Whom? The Role of Gender', *Journal of Communication*, 1976, 26(3), pp. 164–172.

Cantor J.R., Bryant J., Zillmann D., 'Enhancement of Humour Appreciation by Transferred Excitation', *Journal of Personality & Social*

Psychology, 1974, 30(6), pp. 812–21.

Carstensen L.L., Gottman J.M., Levenson R.W., 'Emotional Behavior in Long-Term Marriage', *Psychology and Aging*, 1995, 10(1), pp. 140–49.

Castell P. J., Goldstein J.H., *Social Occasions for Joking: A Cross-Cultural Study*, in Chapman A.J., Foot H.C. (Eds.), *It's a Funny Thing, Humour*, Oxford, Pergamon Press, 1977.

Chapman A.J., 'Social Facilitation of Laughter in Children', *Journal of Experimental Social Psychology*, 1973b, 9(6), pp. 528–41.

Chapman A.J., *Social Aspects of Humorous Laughter*, in Chapman A.J., Foot H.C.(Eds.), *Humour and Laughter: Theory, Research, and Applications*, John Wiley & Sons, 1976, pp. 155–85.

Chapman A.J., Foot H.C., *Humour and Laughter: Theory, Research and Applications*, John Wiley & Sons, 1976.

Chapman A.J., Gadfield N.J., 'Is Sexual Humour Sexist?', *Journal of Communication*, 1976, 26(3), pp. 141–53.

Cheng W., 'Humour in Intercultural Conversation', *Semiotica*, 2003, 146(1–4).

Clarke A., *The Pattern Recognition Theory of Humour*, Pyrrhic House, 2008.

Clouse R.W., Spurgeon K.L., 'Corporate Analysis of Humour', *Psychology: A Journal of Human Behavior*, 1995, 32(3–4), pp. 1–24.

Cohan C.L., Bradbury T.N., 'Negative Life Events, Marital Interaction, and the Longitudinal Course of Newlywed Marriage', *Journal of Personality & Social Psychology*, 1997, 73(1), pp. 114–28.

Collinson D.L., 'Engineering Humour: Masculinity, Joking and Conflict in Shop-Floor Relations', *Organization Studies*, 1988, 9(2), pp. 181–99.

Consalvo C.M., 'Humour in Management: No Laughing Matter', *Humour: International Journal of Humour Research*, 1989, 2(3), pp. 285–97.

Cook K.S., Rice E., *Social Exchange Theory*, in Delamater J. (Ed.), *Handbook of Social Psychology*, New York, Plenum, 2003, pp. 53–76.

Corey M.S., Corey G., *Groups: Process and Practice*, 5th ed., Brooks/Cole, 1997.

Coser R.L., 'Some Social Functions of Laughter: A Study of Humour in a Hospital Setting', *Human Relations*, 1959, 12.

Coser R.L., 'Laughter among Colleagues: A Study of the Functions of

Humour Among the Staff of a Mental Hospital', *Psychiatry*, 1960, 23, pp. 81–95.

Cox J.A., Read R.L., Van Auken P. M., 'Male-Female Differences in Communicating Job-Related Humour: An Exploratory Study', *Humour*, 1990, 3, pp. 287–95.

Craik K.H., Lampert M.D., Nelson A.J., 'Sense of Humour and Styles of Everyday Humorous Conduct', *Humour: International Journal of Humour Research*, 1996, 9(3–4), pp. 273–302.

Crawford M., *Humour in Conversational Context: Beyond Biases in the Study of Gender and Humour*, in UNGER R.K.(Ed.), *Representations: Social Constructions of Gender*, Baywood Publishing, 1989, pp. 155–66.

Crawford M., Gressley D., 'Creativity, Caring, and Context: Women's and Men's Accounts of Humour Preferences and Practices', *Psychology of Women Quarterly*, 1991, 15(2), pp. 217–31.

Creusere M.A., 'A Developmental Test of Theoretical Perspectives on the Understanding of Verbal Irony: Children's Recognition of Allusion and Pragmatic Insincerity', *Metaphor & Symbol*, 2000, 15(1–2), pp. 29–45.

Danzer A., Dale J.A., Klions H.L., *Effect of Exposure to Humorous Stimuli on Induced Depression*, Psychological Reports, 1990, 66 (3, Pt 1), pp. 1027–36.

Davies C., *Ethnic Humour Around the World: A Comparative Analysis*, Indiana University Press, 1990.

De Groot A., Kaplan J., Rosenblatt E., Dews S., Winner E., 'Understanding Versus Discriminating Nonliteral Utterances: Evidence for a Dissociation', *Metaphor & Symbol*, 1995, 10(4), pp. 255–73.

Deal T.E.D., Kennedy A.A., *Corporate Cultures: The Rites and Rituals of Corporate Life*, Addison-Wesley, 1982.

Decker W.H., 'Managerial Humour and Subordinate Satisfaction', *Social Behavior & Personality*, 1987, 15(2), pp. 225–32.

Decker W.H., Rotondo D.M. 'Use of Humour at Work: Predictors and Implications', *Psychological reports*, 1999, 84(3), pp. 961–68.

Deckers L., Carr D.E., 'Cartoons Varying in Low-Level Pain Ratings, Not Aggression Ratings, Correlate Positively with Funniness Ratings',

Motivation & Emotion, 1986, 10(3), pp. 207-16.

Derks P., Gardner J.B., Agarwal R., 'Recall of Innocent and Tendentious Humorous Material', *Humour—International Journal of Humour Research*, 1998, 11(1), pp. 5-19.

Dews S., Winner E., Kaplan J., Rosenblatt E., Hunt M., Lim K., et al., 'Children's Understanding of the Meaning and Functions of Verbal Irony', *Child Development*, 1996, 67(6), pp. 3071-85.

Dillman D.N., Sinclair M.D., Clarck J.R., 'Effects Of Questionnaire Length, Respondent-Friendly Design, and a Difficult Question on Response Rates for Occupant-Addressed Census Mail Surveys', *Public Opinion*, 1993, 57 (3), pp. 289-304.

Dixon N.F., *Humour: A Cognitive Alternative to Stress?*, in Sarason I.G., Spielberger C.D. (Eds.), *Stress and Anxiety*, Hemisphere, 1980, Vol. 7, pp. 281-89.

Doris P., *The Humour Styles Questionnaire: Investigating the Role of Humour in Psychological Well-being*, Unpublished doctoral dissertation, University of Western Ontario, 2004.

Draitser E., 'Comparative Analysis of Russian and American Humour', Meta, 1989, 34(1).

Duncan C.P., Nelson J.E., Frontzak N.L., *The Effect of Humour on Advertising Comprehension*, in Kinnear T.C.(Ed.), *Advances in Consumer Research*, Association for Consumer Research, 1984, pp. 432-37.

Duncan W.J., FeisaL J.P., 'No Laughing Matter: Patterns of Humour in the Workplace', *Organizational Dynamics*, 1989, 17(4), pp. 18-30.

Duncan W.J., Smeltzer L.R., Leap T.L., 'Humour and Work: Applications of Joking Behavior to Management', *Journal of Management*, 1990, 16(2), pp. 255-78.

Dunlop W.P. , Cortina J.M., Vaslow J.B., Burke M.J., 'Meta-Analysis of Experiments with Matched Groups or Repeated Measures Designs', *Psychological Methods*, 1996, 1, pp. 170-77.

Dworkin E.S., Efran J.S., 'The Angered: Their Susceptibility to Varieties of Humour', *Journal of Personality & Social Psychology*, 1967, 6(2), pp. 233-36.

Eastman M., *Enjoyment of Laughter*, Simon and Schuster, 1936.

Epstein S., Smith R., 'Repression and Insight as Related to Reaction to Cartoons', *Journal of Consulting Psychology*, 1956, 20, pp. 391–95.

Ervin-Tripp S.M., Lampert M.D., *Gender Differences in the Construction of Humorous Talk*, in Hall K., Buchholtz M., Moonwomon B. (Eds.), *Locating Power: Proceedings of the Second Berkeley Women and Language Conference*, Berkeley Women and Language Group, Linguistics Department, University of California, 1992, pp. 108–17.

Fabrizi M.S., Pollio H.R., 'A naturalistic study of humorous activity in a third, seventh, and eleventh grade classroom', *Merrill-Palmer Quarterly*, 1987, 33(1), pp. 107–28.

Feinberg L., 'The Secret of Humour', *Maledicta: The International Journal of Verbal Aggression*, 2, 1978.

Feingold A., 'Gender Differences in Mate Selection Preferences: A Test of the Parental Investment Model', *Psychological Bulletin*, 1992, 112(1), pp. 125–39.

Felmlee D.H., 'Fatal Attractions: Affection and Disaffection in Intimate Relationships', *Journal of Social & Personal Relationships*, 1995, 12(2), pp. 295–311.

Ferner R.E., Aronson J.K. 'Laughter and Mirth (Methodical Investigation of Risibility, Therapeutic and Harmful): Narrative Synthesis', *British Medical Journal*, 2013, 347.

Fierman J., 'The Contingency Work Force', *Fortune*, 1994, 129(2).

Fine G.A., *Sociological Approaches to the Study of Humour*, in McGhee P.E., Goldstein J.H.(Eds.), *Handbook of Humour Research*, Springer-Verlag, 1983, Vol. 2, 4(1), pp. 159–81.

Forabosco G., 'Cognitive Aspects of the Humour Process: The Concept of Incongruity', *Humour: International Journal of Humour Research*, 1992, 5(1–2), pp. 45–68.

Forester J., 'Responding to Critical Moments with Humour, Recognition, and Hope', *Negotiation Journal*, 2004, 20(2), pp. 221–37.

Fraley B., Aron A., 'The Effect of a Shared Humorous Experience on Closeness in Initial Encounters', *Personal Relationships*, 2004, 11(1), pp. 61–78.

Fredrickson B.L., 'What Good Are Positive Emotions?', *Review of General Psychology*, 1998, 2(3), pp. 300–19.

Freud S., 'Humour', *International Journal of Psychoanalysis*, 1928, 9, pp. 1–6.

Freud S., *Jokes and Their Relation to the Unconscious*, Norton, 1960 [1905].

Gabriel Y., Fineman S., Sims D., *Organizing and Organizations: An Introduction*, 2nd Ed. Sage, 2000.

Galesic M., Bonjak M., 'Effects of Questionnaire Length on Participation and Indicators of Response Quality in a Web Survey', *Public Opinion Quarterly*, 2009, 73(2), pp. 349–60.

Garancini S., *Humor and Leadership: A Subordinates' Perception Analysis*, Unpublished MSc Thesis, Bocconi University, 2014.

Gelb B.D., Zinkhan G.M., 'Humour and Advertising Effectiveness After Repeated Exposures to a Radio Commerical', *Journal of Advertising*, 1986, 15(2), pp. 15–20.

Gkorezis P., Hatzithomas L., Petridou E. 'The Impact of Leader's Humour on Employees' Psychological Empowerment: The Moderating Role of Tenure', *Journal of Managerial Issues*, 23(1), pp. 83–95

Gladstein D.L., 'Groups in Context: A Model of Task Group Effectiveness', *Administrative Science Quarterly*, 1984, 29.

Godkewitsch M., *Physiological and Verbal Indices of Arousal in Rated Humour*, in Chapman A.J., Foot H.C. (Eds.), *Humour and Laughter: Theory, Research, and Applications*, John Wiley & Sons, 1976, pp. 117–38.

Goffman E., *Interaction Ritual: Essays on Face-to-Face Behavior*, Anchor Books, 1967.

Goldstein J.H., Harman J., McGhee P. E., Karasik R., 'Test of An Information Processing Model of Humour: Physiological Response Changes During Problem and Riddle-Solving', *Journal of General Psychology*, 1975, 92(1), pp. 59–68.

Goodchilds J.D., *On Being Witty: Causes, Correlates and Consequences*, in Goldstein J., McGhee P. (Eds.), *The Psychology of Humour*, Academic Press, 1972.

Goodman L., *Gender and Humour: Positions, Perspectives, Gender and Humour*, in Bonner F.et al. (Eds.)., *Imagining Women: Cultural Representations and Gender*, Polity Press, 1992, pp. 286–300.

Goodman R.A., Goodman L.P., 'Some Management Issues in Temporary Systems: A Study of Professional Development and Manpower—The Theater Case', *Administrative Science Quarterly*, 1976, 21.

Gottman J.M., 'The Roles of Conflict Engagement, Escalation, and Avoidance in Marital Interaction: A Longitudinal View of Five Types of Couples', *Journal of Consulting & Clinical Psychology*, 1993, 61(1), pp. 6–15.

Gottman J.M., Coan J., Carrere S., Swanson C., 'Predicting Marital Happiness and Stability From Newlywed Interactions', *Journal of Marriage and the Family*, 1998, 60, pp. 5–22.

Greig J.Y.T., *The Psychology of Laughter and Comedy*, Dodd, Mead, 1923.

Groch A.S., 'Generality of Response to Humour and Wit in Cartoons, Jokes, Stories, and Photographs', *Psychological Reports*, 1974, 35, pp. 835–38.

Grotjahn M., *Beyond Laughter: A Psychoanalytical Approach to Humour*, McGraw Hill, 1957.

Grotjahn M., *Beyond Laughter: Humour and the Subconscious*, McGraw-Hill, 1966.

Grugulis I., 'Nothing Serious? Candidates' Use of Humour in Management Training', *Human Relations*, 2002, 55(4), pp. 387–406.

Gruner C.R., *Wit and Humour in Mass Communication*, in Chapman A.J., Foot H.C. (Eds)., *Humour and Laughter: Theory, Research, and Applications*, John Wiley & Sons, 1976, pp. 287–311.

Gruner C.R., *Understanding Laughter: The Workings of Wit and Humour*, Nelson-Hall, 1978.

Gruner C.R., *The Game of Humour: A Comprehensive Theory of Why We Laugh*, Transaction Publishers, 1997.

Hackman J.R., *The Design of Work Team*, in LORSH J.W.(Ed.), *Handbook of Organizational Behaviour*, Prentice Hall, 1987.

Harre R., Lamb R. (Eds), *The Encyclopedic Dictionary of Psychology*, The MIT Press, 1983.

Hatch M.J., Ehrlich S.B., 'Spontaneous Humour as An Indicator of Paradox and Ambiguity in Organizations', *Organization Studies*, 1993, 14(4), pp. 505–26.

Hay J., 'Functions of Humour in the Conversations of Men and Women',

Journal of Pragmatics, 2000, 32(6), pp. 709–42.

Hebb D.O., 'Drives and the C.N.S. (Conceptual Nervous System)', *Psychological Review*, 1955, 62, pp. 243–54.

Hemmasi M., Graf L.A., Russ G.S., 'Gender-Related Jokes in the Workplace: Sexual Humour or Sexual Harassment?', *Journal of Applied Social Psychology*, 1994, 24(12), pp. 1114–28.

Henkin B., Fish J.M., 'Gender and Personality Differences in the Appreciation of Cartoon Humour', *Journal of Psychology*, 1986, 120(2), pp. 157–75.

Hertzler J., *Laughter: A Socio-Scientific Analysis*, Exposition Press, 1970.

Herzberg F., *Work and the Nature of Man*, World Publishing, 1966.

Hiranandani N.A. 'Humour Styles, Gelotophobia and Self-esteem: A Comparative Study Between the Chinese and the Indians', *City University of Honk Kong*, 2010.

Hobbes T., *Leviathan*, 1651.

Hofstede G., *Humour Across Cultures: An Appetizer*, Wageningen University, 2006.

Holmes D.S., 'Sensing Humour: Latency and Amplitude of Response Related to Mmpi Profiles', *Journal of Consulting & Clinical Psychology*, 1969, 33(3), pp. 296–301.

Holmes J., Marra M., 'Having a Laugh at Work: How Humour Contributes to Workplace Culture', *Journal of Pragmatics*, 2002a, 34(12), pp. 1683–710.

Holmes J., Marra M., 'Over the Edge? Subversive Humour between Colleagues and Friends', *Humour: International Journal of Humour Research*, 2002b, 15(1), pp. 65–87.

Horner I.B., *The Book of the Discipline (Vinaya-pitaka)*, Vol. 3 (Sutta-vibhanga), London: Pali Text Society, 1983.

Hurn B.J., 'Building Multinational Teams: The Challenge', *International Journal of Value-Based Management*, 1997, 10(3).

Isen A.M., Daubman K.A., 'The Influence of Affect on Categorization', *Journal of Personality and Social Psychology*, 1984, 47, pp. 1206–17.

Isen A.M., Johnson M.M.S., Mertz E., Robinson G.F., 'The Influence of Positive Affect on the Unusualness of Word Associations', *Journal of Personality and Social Psychology*, 1985, 48, pp. 1413–26.

Isen A.M., Daubman K.A., Nowicki G.P., 'Positive Affect Facilitates Creative Problem Solving', *Journal of Personality and Social Psychology*, 1987, 52, pp. 1122–31.

Isen A.M., *Positive Affect and Decision Making*, in Lewis M., Haviland J.M.(Eds.), *Handbook of Emotions*, Guilford, 1993, pp. 261–77.

Ivancevich J.M., Matteson M.T., *Organizational Behavior and Management*, 4th Ed., McGraw-Hill, 1996.

Jenkins M., *What's So Funny?: Joking Among Women*, in Bremner S., Caskey N., Moonwomon B.(Eds.), *Proceedings of the First Berkeley Women and Language Conference*, Women and Language Group Berkeley, 1985, pp. 135–151.

Johnson A.K., Anderson E.A., *Stress and Arousal*, in Cacioppo J.T., Tassinary L.G. (Eds.)., *Principles of Psychophysiology: Physical, Social, and Inferential Elements*, Cambridge University Press, 1990, pp. 216–52.

Jones J.M., Harris P. E., 'Psychophysiological Correlates of Cartoon Humour Appreciation', *Proceedings of the Annual Convention of the American Psychological Association*, 1971, 6, pp. 381–82.

Kaiser H., 'A Second Generation Little Jiffy', *Psychometrika*, 1970, 35, pp. 401–15.

Kaiser H., 'An Index of Factorial Simplicity', *Psychometrika*, 1974, 39, pp. 31–36.

Kambouropoulou P., 'Individual Differences in the Sense of Humour', *American Journal of Psychology*, 1926, 37, pp. 268–78.

Kane T.R., Suls J., Tedeschi J.T., *Humour as A Tool of Social Interaction*, in Chapman A.J., Foot H.C.(Eds.), *It's a Funny Thing, Humour*, Pergamon Press, 1977, pp. 13–16.

Kaplan R.M., Pascoe G.C., 'Humorous Lectures and Humorous Examples: Some Effects Upon Comprehension and Retention', *Journal of Educational Psychology*, 1977, 69(1), pp. 61–65.

Keith-Spiegel P., *Early Conceptions of Humour: Varieties and Issues*, in Goldstein J.H., McGhee P. E.(Eds.), *The Psychology of Humour: Theoretical Perspectives and Empirical Issues*, Academic Press, 1972, pp. 3–39.

Keltner D., Young R.C., Heerey E.A., Oemig C., Monarch N.D., 'Teasing in Hierarchical and Intimate Relations', *Journal of Personality and Social Psychology*, 1998, 75(5), pp. 1231–47.

Kenny D.T., 'The Contingency of Humour Appreciation on the Stimulus-Confirmation of Joke-Ending Expectations', *Journal of Abnormal & Social Psychology*, 1955, 51, pp. 644–48.

Kintsch W., Bates E., 'Recognition Memory for Statements from a Classroom Lecture', *Journal of Experimental Psychology: Human Learning and Memory*, 1977, 3, pp. 150–59.

Klein A.J., 'Humour Comprehension and Humour Appreciation of Cognitively Oriented Humour: A Study of Kindergarten Children', *Child Study Journal*, 1985, 15(4), pp. 223–35.

Kline L.W., 'The Psychology of Humour', *The American Journal of Psychology*, 1907, 18, 4.

Koestler A., *The Act of Creation*, Hutchinson, 1964.

Kramarae C., *Women and Men Speaking*, Newbury House, 1981.

Kurtzberg T.R., Naquin C.E., Belkin L.Y. 'Humour as a Relationship-Building Tool in Online Negotiations', *International Journal of Conflict Management*, 20(4), pp. 377–97.

La Gaipa J.J., *The Effects of Humour on the Flow of Social Conversation*, in Chapman A.J., Foot H.C.(Eds)., *It's a Funny Thing, Humour*, Pergamon Press, 1977, pp. 421–27.

Lampert M.D., Ervin-Tripp S.M., *Exploring Paradigms: The Study of Gender and Sense of Humour Near the End of the 20th Century*, in Ruch W.(Ed.), *The Sense of Humour: Explorations of a Personality Characteristic*, Walter de Gruyter, 1998, pp. 231–70.

La Mar L.A., Darwin G., 'Solving the Quandary between Questionnaire Length and Response Rate in Educational Research', *Research in Higher Education*, 1982, 17(3), pp. 231–40.

Lakoff R., *Language and Woman's Place,* Harper Colophon, 1975.

Lauer R.H., Lauer J.C., Kerr S.T., 'The Long-Term Marriage: Perceptions of Stability and Satisfaction', *International Journal of Aging & Human Development*, 1990, 31(3), pp. 189–95.

Lazarus R.S., Folkman S., *Stress, Appraisal, and Coping*, Springer, 1984.

Leak G.K., 'Effects of Hostility Arousal and Aggressive Humour on Catharsis and Humour Preference', *Journal of Personality & Social*

Psychology, 1974, 30(6), pp. 736–40.

Lefcourt H.M., *Humour: The Psychology of Living Buoyantly*, Kluwer Academic, 2001.

Lefcourt H.M., Martin R.A., *Humour and Life Stress: Antidote to Adversity*, Springer-Verlag, 1986.

Levin J. *Humour*, in Pettijohn T.(Eds)., *The Encyclopedic Dictionary of Psychology*, Guilford, Dushkin, 1986.

Locke E.A., *The Motivation to Work: What We Know*, in Maehr M.L., Pintrich P. R. (Eds)., *Advances in Motivation and Achievement*, Jai Press, 1997, 10. Long D.L., Graesser A.C., 'Wit and Humour in Discourse Processing', *Discourse Processes*, 1988, 11(1), pp. 35–60. Mann R.D., 'Dimensions of Individual Performance in Small Groups under Task and Socio-Emotional Conditions', *Journal of Abnormal and Social Psychology*, 1961, 62.

Mannell R.C., Mcmahon L., 'Humour as Play: It's Relationship to Psychological Well-being During the Course of a Day', *Leisure Sciences*, 1982, 5(2), pp. 143–55.

Marlowe L., *A Sense of Humour*, in: Unger R.K. (Eds)., *Representations: Social Constructions of Gender*, Baywood, 1989, pp. 145–54.

Martin D.M., 'Humour in Middle Management: Women Negotiating the Paradoxes of Organizational Life', *Journal of Applied Communication Research*, 2004, 32(2), pp. 147–70.

Martin R.A., 'Humour, Laughter, and Physical Health: Methodological Issues and Research Findings', *Psychological Bulletin*, 2001, 127(4), pp. 504–19.

Martin R.A., Kuiper N.A., 'Daily Occurrence of Laughter: Relationships with Age, Gender, and Type A Personality', *Humour—International Journal of Humour Research*, 1999, 12(4), pp. 355–84.

Martin R.A., Kuiper N.A., Olinger L.J., Dance K.A. 'Humour, Coping with Stress, Self-Concept, and Psychological Well-being', *Humour—International Journal of Humour Research*, 1993, 6(1), pp. 89–104.

Martin R.A., Puhlik-Doris P., Larsen G., Gray J., Weir K. 'Individual Differences in Uses of Humour and Their Relation to Psychological Well-being: Development of the Humour Styles Questionnaire', *Journal of Research in Personality*, 2003, 37(1), pp. 48–75.

Martin R.A., *The Psychology of Humour: An Integrative Approach*, Burlington, Elsevier, 2007.

MARTINEAU W.H., *A Model of the Social Functions of Humour*, in GOLDSTEIN J.H., McGhee P. E. (Eds)., *The Psychology of Humour: Theoretical Perspectives and Empirical Issues*, Academic Press, 1972, pp. 101–25.

Maslow A.H., *Motivation and Personality*, Harper, 1954.

McCauley C., Woods K., Coolidge C., Kulick W., 'More Aggressive Cartoons are Funnier', *Journal of Personality & Social Psychology*, 1983, 44(4), pp. 817–23.

McGhee P. E., 'Cognitive Development and Children's Comprehension of Humour', *Child Development*, 1971a, 42(1), pp. 123–38.

McGhee P. E., 'The Role of Operational Thinking in Children's Comprehension and Appreciation of Humour', *Child Development*, 1971b, 42(3), pp. 733–44.

McGhee P. E., 'Cognitive Mastery and Children's Humour', *Psychological Bulletin*, 1974, 81(10), pp. 721–30.

McGhee P. E. (Ed)., *Humour: Its Origin and Development*, W.H. Freeman, 1979.

McGhee P. E., *Humour Development: Toward a Life Span Approach*, in McGhee P. E., Goldstein J.H.(Eds.), *Handbook of Humour Research*, New York, Springer-Verlag, 1983a, 1, pp. 109–34.

McGhee P. E., *The Negative Side of Humour: Put-Down Jokes*, www.laughterremedy.com

McGuire W.J., *Personality and Susceptibility to Social Influence*, in Borgatta E.F., Lambert W.W.(Eds)., *Handbook of Personality Theory and Research*, Rand McNally, 1968.

Mednick S.A., 'The Associative Basis of the Creative Process', *Psychological Review*, 1962, 69, pp. 220–32.

Mettee D.R., Hrelec E.S., Wilkens P. C., 'Humour As An Interpersonal Asset and Liability', *Journal of Social Psychology*, 1971, 85(1), pp. 51–64.

Meyer J.C., 'Humour in Member Narratives: Uniting and Dividing at Work', *Western Journal of Communication*, 1997, 61(2), pp. 188–208.

Middleton R., 'Negro and White Reactions to Racial Humour',

Sociometry, 1959, 22, pp. 175–83.

Moran C.C., 'Short-Term Mood Change, Perceived Funniness, and the Effect of Humour Stimuli', *Behavioral Medicine*, 1996, 22(1), pp. 32–38.

Morreall J.(Ed.), *The Philosophy of Laughter and Humour*, State University of New York Press, 1987.

Mueller C.W., Donnerstein E., 'Film-Induced Arousal and Aggressive Behavior', *Journal of Social Psychology*, 1983, 119(1), pp. 61–67.

Mulkay M., *On Humour: Its Nature and Its Place in Modern Society*, Basil Blackwell, 1988.

Mulkay M., Clark C., Pinch T., 'Laughter and the Profit Motive: The Use of Humour in a Photographic Shop', *Humour: International Journal of Humour Research*, 1993, 6(2), pp. 163–93.

Nelson A., 'Gender Gestures', *Psychology Today*, 29 October 2010. http://www.psychologytoday.com/blog/he-speaks-she-speaks/201010/gendered-gestures

Nerhardt G., *Operationalization of Incongruity in Humour Research: A Critique and Suggestions*, in Chapman A.J., Foot H.C. (Eds.), *It's a Funny Thing, Humour*, Pergamon Press, 1977, pp. 47–51.

Nevo O., 'Appreciation and Production of Humour As An Expression of Aggression: A Study of Jews and Arabs in Israel', *Journal of Cross-Cultural Psychology*, 1984, 15.

Newman M.G., Stone A.A., 'Does Humour Moderate the Effects of Experimentally Induced Stress?', *Annals of Behavioral Medicine*, 1996, 18(2), pp. 101–9.

Newstrom J.W., Davis K., *Organizational Behavior: Human Behavior at Work*, McGraw-Hill, 2001.

Norman R., 'When What is Said is Important: A Comparison of Expert and Attractive Sources', *Journal of Experimental Social Psychology*, 1976, 12.

O'Connell W.E., *Freudian Humour: The Eupsychia of Everyday Life*, in Chapman A.J., Foot H.C. (Eds)., *Humour and Laughter: Theory, Research, and Applications*, John Wiley & Sons, 1976, pp. 313–29.

O'Connell W.E., *Humour*, in Corsini R.J. (Ed.), *Encyclopedia of Psychology*, Wiley & Sons, 1984/1994.

O'Quin K., Aronoff J., 'Humour As A Technique of Social Influence', *Social Psychology Quarterly*, 1981, 44(4), pp. 349–57.

O'Quin K., Derks P., *Humour and Creativity: A Review of the Empirical Literature*, in Runco M.A. (Ed.), *The Creativity Handbook*, Cresskill, Hampton Press, 1997, 1, pp. 227–56.

Oring E., 'Humour and the Suppression of Sentiment', *Humour—International Journal of Humour Research*, 1994, 7(1), pp. 7–26.

Parrott W.G., Gleitman H., 'Infants' Expectations in Play: The Joy of Peek-a-boo', *Cognition & Emotion*, 1989, 3(4), pp. 291–311.

Philbrick K., *The Use of Humour and Effective Leadership Styles*, Doctoral dissertation, University of Florida, 1989.

Piaget J., *Play, Dreams and Intelligence in Children*, Norton, 1962.

Pihulyk A., 'Working with Humour', *The Canadian Manager*, 27(3), pp. 21–22

Pizzini F., 'Communication Hierarchies in Humour: Gender Differences in the Obstetrical /Gynecological Setting', *Discourse in Society*, 1991, 2(4), pp. 477–88.

Pollio H.R., Mers R.W., X 'Predictability and the Appreciation of Comedy', *Bulletin of the Psychonomic Society*, 1991, 4(4-A), pp. 229–32.

Prerost F.J., 'Changing Patterns in the Response to Humorous Sexual Stimuli: Sex Roles and Expression of Sexuality', *Social Behavior& Personality*, 1983, 11(1), pp. 23–28.

Prerost F.J., Brewer R.E., 'Humour Content Preferences and the Relief of Experimentally Aroused Aggression', *Journal of Social Psychology*, 1977, 103(2), pp. 225–31.

Priest R.F., Swain J.E., 'Humour and Its Implications For Leadership Effectiveness', *Humour—International Journal of Humour Research*, 2002, 15(2), pp. 169–89.

Provine R.R., *Laughter: A Scientific Investigation*, Penguin, 2000.

Provine R.R., Fischer K.R., 'Laughing, Smiling, and Talking: Relation to Sleeping and Social Context in Humans', *Ethology*, 1989, 83(4), pp. 295–305.

Raskin V., *Semantic Mechanisms of Humour*, D. Reidel, 1985.

Raskin V. (Ed.), *The Primer of Humour Research*, Mouton De Gruyter, 2007.

Robinson D.T., Smith-Lovin L., 'Getting a Laugh: Gender, Status, and Humour in Task Discussions', *Social Forces*, 2001, 80(1), pp. 123–58.

Roeckelein J.E., *The Psychology of Humour*, Greenwood Press, 2001.

Roeckelein J.E., *The Psychology of Humour: A Reference Guide and Annotated Bibliography*, Greenwood Press, 2002.

Rosenthal R., *Meta-Analytic Procedures for Social Research*, Sage, 1991.

Rothbart M.K., *Incongruity, Problem-Solving and Laughter*, in Chapman A.J., Foot H.C. (Eds)., *Humour and Laughter: Theory, Research, and Applications*, Wiley & Sons, 1976, pp. 37–54.

Rothwell S., 'Managing Conflict', *Manager Update*, 1996, 7(4).

Ruch W., *Assessment of Appreciation of Humour: Studies With the 3 WD Humour Test*, in Spielberger C.D., Butcher J.N. (Eds)., *Advances in Personality Assessment*, Lawrence Erlbaum Associates, 1992, Vol. 9, pp. 27–75.

Ruch W., Forabosco G., 'A Cross-Cultural Study of Humour Appreciation: Italy and Germany', *Humour—International Journal of Humour Research*, 1996, 9(1), 1–18.

Ruch W., Hehl F.J., *A Two-Mode Model of Humour Appreciation: Its Relation to Aesthetic Appreciation and Simplicity-Complexity of Personality*, in Ruch W. (Ed.), *The Sense of Humour: Explorations of a Personality Characteristic*, Walter de Gruyter, 1998, pp. 109–42.

Ruch W., McGhee P. E., Hehl F.J., 'Age Differences in the Enjoyment of Incongruity-Resolution and Nonsense Humour During Adulthood', *Psychology & Aging*, 1990, 5(3), pp. 348–55.

Ruch W., Ott C., Accoce J., Bariaud F., 'Cross-National Comparison of Humour Categories: France and Germany', *Humour—International Journal of Humour Research*, 1991, 4(3–4), pp. 391–414.

Ruch W., Proyer R.T., Weber M., 'Humour as Character Strength among the Elderly: Empirical Findings on Age-Related Changes and Its Contribution to Satisfaction with Life', *Zeitschrift für Gerontologie und Geriatrie*, 2010, 43, pp. 13–18.

Rust J., Goldstein J., 'Humour in Marital Adjustment', *Humour—International Journal of Humour Research*, 1989, 2(3), pp. 217–23.

Sampietro M., *Use and Effects of Humor in International Teams: A Cross Country Comparison*, EGEA, 2013.

Sanderson C.A., *Health Psychology*, Wiley & Sons, 2004.

Schachter S., Wheeler L., 'Epinephrine, Chlorpromazine, and Amusement', *Journal of Abnormal & Social Psychology*, 1962, 65(2), pp. 121–28.

Schaier A.H., Cicirelli V.G., 'Age Differences in Humour Comprehension and Appreciation in Old Age', *Journal of Gerontology*, 1976, 31(5), pp. 577–82.

Schmidt S.R., 'Effects of Humour on Sentence Memory', *Journal of Experimental Psychology: Learning, Memory, & Cognition*, 1994, 20(4), pp. 953–67.

Schmidt S.R., 'The Humour Effect: Differential Processing and Privileged Retrieval', *Memory*, 2002, 10(2), pp. 127–38.

Schmidt S.R., Williams A.R., 'Memory for Humorous Cartoons', *Memory & Cognition*, 2001, 29(2), pp. 305–11.

Schmitz J.R., 'Humour as a Pedagogical Tool in Foreign Language and Translation Courses', *International Journal of Humour Research*, 2002, 15(1).

Sechrest L., Fay T.L., Zaidi S.M.H., 'Problems of Translation in Cross Cultural Research', *Journal of Cross-Cultural Psychology*, 1972, 3(1), pp. 41–56.

Senior B., 'Team Performance: Using Repertory Grid Technique to Gain a View From the Inside', *Team Performance Management*, 1997, 3(1), pp. 33–39.

Senior B., Swailes B., 'Inside Management Teams: Developing a Teamwork Survey Instrument', *British Journal of Management*, 2007, 18(2), pp. 138–53.

Shammi P., Stuss D.T., 'The Effects of Normal Aging on Humour Appreciation', *Journal of the International Neuropsychological Society*, 2003, 9(6), pp. 855–63.

Shultz T.R., 'The Role of Incongruity and Resolution in Children's Appreciation of Cartoon Humour', *Journal of Experimental Child Psychology*, 1972, 13(3), pp. 456–77.

Shultz T.R., *A Cognitive-Developmental Analysis of Humour*, in Chapman A.J., Foot H.C. (Eds)., *Humour and Laughter: Theory, Research, and Applications*, Wiley & Sons, 1976, pp. 11–36.

Shultz T.R., Horibe F., 'Development of the Appreciation of Verbal Jokes', *Developmental Psychobiology*, 1974, 10, pp. 13–20.

Shurcliff A., 'Judged Humour, Arousal, and the Relief Theory', *Journal of Personality & Social Psychology*, 1968, 8(4), pp. 360–63.

Singer D.L., Gollob H.F., Levine J., 'Mobilization of Inhibitions and the Enjoyment of Aggressive Humour', *Journal of Personality*, 1967, 35(4), pp. 562–69.

Smith A., *The Theory of Moral Sentiments*, 1759.

Smith J.E., Waldorf V.A., Trembath D.L., 'Single White Male Looking For Thin, Very Attractive...', *Sex Roles*, 1990, 23(11/12), pp. 675–85.

Smith W.J., Harrington K.V., Neck C.P., 'Resolving Conflict with Humour in a Diversity Context', *Journal of Managerial Psychology*, 2000, 15(6).

Snyder C.R., Harris C., Anderson J.R., Holleran S.A., Irving L.M., Sigmon S.T., Yoshinobu L., Langelle C., Harney P. , 'The Will and the Ways: Development and Validation of an Individual-Differences Measure of Hope', *Journal of Personality and Social Psychology*, 1991, 60, pp. 570–85.

Spencer H., 'The Physiology of Laughter', *Macmillan's Magazine*, 1860, 1, pp. 395–402.

Sprecher S., Regan P. C., 'Liking Some Things (in some people) More than Others: Partner Preferences in Romantic Relationships and Friendships', *Journal of Social & Personal Relationships*, 2002, 19(4), pp. 463–81.

Stanley J.T., Lohani M., Isaacowitz, D.M., 'Age-Related Differences in Judgments of Inappropriate Behavior are Related to Humour Style Preferences', *Psychology and Aging*, 2014, 29, 528–41.

Stotlan D E., *The Psychology of Hope*, Jossey-Bass, 1969.

Strickland J.F., 'The Effect of Motivational Arousal on Humour Preferences', *Journal of Abnormal and Social Psychology*, 1959, 59, pp. 278–81.

Strombom T.A., *Humour and the Problem Solving Behavior of Married Couples*, Doctoral dissertation: Virginia Polytechnic Institute and State University, 1989.

Sullivan K., Winner E., Hopfield N., 'How Children Tell a Lie from a

Joke: The Role of Second-Order Mental State Attributions', *British Journal of Developmental Psychology*, 1995, 13(2), pp. 191–204.

Suls J.M., *A Two-Stage Model for the Appreciation of Jokes and Cartoons: An Information- Processing Analysis*, in Goldstein J.H., McGhee P. E. (Eds)., *The Psychology of Humour: Theoretical Perspectives and Empirical Issues*, Academic Press, 1972, pp. 81–100.

Suls J.M., *Cognitive Processes in Humour Appreciation*, in McGhee P. E., Goldstein J.H. (Eds.), *Handbook of Humour Research*, New York, Springer-Verlag, 1983, Vol. 1: Basic Issues, pp. 39–57.

Svebak S., Martin R.A., Holmen J., 'The Prevalence of Sense of Humour in a Large, Unselected County Population in Norway: Relations with Age, Sex, and Some Health Indicators', *Humour—International Journal of Humour Research*, 2004, 17(1–2), pp. 121–34.

Tabachnick B.G., Fidell L.S., *Using Multivariate Analysis*, Allyn and Bacon, 2001.

Tannenbaum S.I., Beard R.L., Salas E., *Team Building and Its Influence on Team Effectiveness: An Examination of Conceptual and Empirical Developments*, in Kelly K.(Ed.), *Issues, Theory and Research in Industrial/Organizational Psychology*, Elsevier, 1992.

Terrion J.L., Ashforth B.E., 'From "I" to "We": The Role of Put-Down Humour and Identity in the Development of a Temporary Group', *Human Relations*, 2002, 55(1), pp. 55–88.

Terry R.L., Ertel S.L., 'Exploration of Individual Differences in Preferences for Humour', *Psychological Reports*, 1974, 34(3, Pt 2), pp. 1031–37.

Tieken H., Schokker G., *Vorstelijke Humour: Driekluchtenuit het klassieke India*, E.J. Brill, 1991.

Traylor G., 'Joking in a Bush Camp', *Human Relations*, 1973, 26(4), pp. 479–86.

Ullian J.A., 'Joking at Work', *Journal of Communication*, 1976, 26(3), pp. 129–33.

Ullmann L.P., Lim D.T., 'Case History Material as a Source of the Identification of Patterns of Response to Emotional Stimuli in a Study of Humour', *Journal of Consulting Psychology*, 1962, 26(3), pp. 221–25.

Vaillant G.E., 'Adaptive Mental Mechanisms: Their Role in a Positive Psychology', *American Psychologist*, 2000, 55(1), pp. 89–98.

Vecchio R.P., Justin J.E., Pearce C.L. 'The Influence of Leader Humour on Relationships between Leader Behavior and Followers Outcomes', *Journal of Managerial Issues*, 1(2), pp. 171–194.

Vettin J., Todt D., 'Laughter in Conversation: Features of Occurrence and Acoustic Structure', *Journal of Nonverbal Behavior*, 2004, 28(2), pp. 93–115.

Vilaythong A.P., Arnau R.C., Rosen D.H., Mascaro N., 'Humour and hope: Can humour increase hope?', *Humour—International Journal of Humour Research*, 2003, 16(1), pp. 79–89.

Vinton K.L., 'Humour in the Workplace: It is More Than Telling Jokes', *Small Group Behavior*, 1989, 20(2), pp. 151–66.

Vroom V., *Work and Motivation*, Wiley & Sons, 1964.

Vuorela T., 'Laughing Matters: A Case Study of Humour in Multicultural Business Negotiations', *Negotiation Journal*, 2005, 21(1), pp. 105–30.

Waters D., 'Laughter across the Great Wall: A Comparison of Chinese and Western Humour', *Journal of the Hong Kong Branch of the Royal Asiatic Society*, 1998, 38.

Whitt J.K., Prentice N.M., 'Cognitive Processes in the Development of Children's Enjoyment and Comprehension of Joking Riddles', *Developmental Psychology*, 1977, 13(2), pp. 129–36.

Wickberg D., *The Senses of Humour: Self and Laughter in Modern America*, Cornell University Press, 1998.

Wilson D.W., Molleston J.L., 'Effects of Sex and Type of Humour on Humour Appreciation', *Journal of Personality Assessment*, 1981, 45(1), pp. 90–96.

Wilson W., 'Sex Differences in Response to Obscenities and Bawdy Humour', *Psychological Reports*, 1975, 37(3, Pt 2), p. 1074.

Winick C., 'The Social Contexts of Humour', *Journal of Communication*, 1976, 26, pp. 124–28.

Winner E., Windmueller G., Rosenblatt E., Bosco L., Best E., Gardner H., 'Making Sense of Literal and Nonliteral Falsehood', *Metaphor & Symbolic Activity*, 1987, 2(1), pp. 13–32.

Wyer R.S., *Social Comprehension and Judgment: The Role of Situation Models, Narratives, and Implicit Theories*, Lawrence Erlbaum Associates, 2004.

Wyer R.S., Collins J.E., 'A Theory of Humour Elicitation', *Psychological Review*, 1992, 99(4), pp. 663–88.

Yalisove D., 'The Effect of Riddle Structure on Children's Comprehension of Riddles', *Developmental Psychology*, 1978, 14(2), pp. 173–80.

Yovetich N.A., Dale J.A., Hudak M.A., 'Benefits of Humour in Reduction of Threat Induced Anxiety', *Psychological Reports*, 1990, 66(1), pp. 51–58.

Zigler E., Levine J., Gould L., 'Cognitive Processes in the Development of Children's Appreciation of Humour', *Child Development*, 1966, 37(3), pp. 507–18.

Zillmann D., Bryant J., 'Retaliatory Equity as a Factor in Humour Appreciation', *Journal of Experimental Social Psychology*, 1974, 10(5), pp. 480–88.

Zillmann D., Cantor J.R., 'A Disposition Theory of Humour and Mirth', in Ziv A.J., 'Facilitating Effects of Humour on Creativity', *Journal of Educational Psychology*, 1976, 68(3), pp. 318–22.

Ziv A., 'Humour's Role in Married Life', *Humour—International Journal of Humour Research*, 1988a, 1(3), pp. 223–29.

Ziv A. (Ed.), *National Styles of Humour*, Greenwood Press, 1998.

Ziv A., Gadish O., 'Humour and Marital satisfaction', *Journal of Social Psychology*, 1989, 129(6), pp. 759–68.